AF335537

Death Did Us Part
A Practical Guide
When A Loved One Has Died

Always remember the good times —
Michael Burns
1-12-2010

Michael D. Burns

SEA STAR PUBLISHING
P.O. Box 98457
Des Moines, Washington 98198-0457
www.SeaStarPublishing.com

Copyright © 2006 by Michael D. Burns

Published by:
Sea Star Publishing
P.O. Box 98457
Des Moines WA 98198-0457

Website - http://www.SeaStarPublishing.com
Email - orders@SeaStarPublishing.com

All rights reserved. No part of this book may be reproduced or transmitted in any form or by any electronic or mechanical means including information storage and retrieval systems without permission in writing from the publisher, except by a reviewer, who may quote passages in a review. The original purchaser of this book may photocopy individual pages to assist in accomplishing the tasks discussed in the book.

Printed in the United States of America
by Gorham Printing, www.gorhamprinting.com

ISBN-13: 978-0-9762982-0-5
ISBN-10: 0-9762982-0-1

Library of Congress Control Number: 2005907034

Cover photo by Michael D. Burns
Photo of Author by Vickie Burns
Cover production by Paul Wilkin-www.GargoyleDesign.com

Disclaimer

This book is designed to provide a wide range of information in an abbreviated manner. It is based on the author's experiences. It is not the purpose of this book to print all information regarding the subject matter; but to amplify, complement, and supplement other texts.

It is sold with the understanding that the author and publisher are not engaged in rendering legal, accounting, financial, or other professional services.

The author and Sea Star Publishing shall have neither liability nor responsibility to any person or entity with respect to any loss or damage caused, directly or indirectly, by the information contained or not contained in this book.

We assume no responsibility for errors, omissions, inaccuracies, or any inconsistency herein.

Dollar amounts should be considered to have changed by date of publication. Check with advisors, and current tax and legal publications, for current dollar amounts.

If legal or other expert assistance is required, the services of a competent professional should be sought.

Unlimited Guarantee

We guarantee your satisfaction.

You may return your book to the publisher if you are not satisfied, and your book purchase price will be refunded.

Acknowledgements

*My sincere thanks go to family and friends
who so generously contributed to the writing
of this book:*

Vickie Burns
Leanne Burns
Randall Burns

Eileen Geller and her mom, Ruth
Edward Meyer and his mom, Annette
Beverly Loeffler and her mom, Hazel Anderson

Rabbi Ted Stainman
Samuel Sotiros, CPA
Marilyn Bickford
John Ramsey

Granddad David and
Grandma Connie Parker
and the family cabin
on Flowing Lake

Dedication

To my wife Vickie, my best friend and soul mate for over 23 years, and the best teacher I've ever known. Thank you for letting me help Mom in her time of need, and encouraging me to write it down.

To my children Ben and Leanne, both of whom I couldn't be more proud, as Ben graduates with his A.A. and works on the cars he loves, and as Leanne, my Renaissance Girl, attends Washington State University.

And to my mom Bernice Anne, who is loved by everyone who knows her, and for her strength and willingness to do what needed to be done.

Introduction - How To Use This Book

This book is easy for you to use. Each page is one task or topic.

First, read the *Contents* pages, which will be your "master checklist". As you read, you will find tasks that you know need immediate attention. I suggest you draw a star with a pencil on the line next to the page number. This will help identify your main concerns.

Work on just one or two pages at a time. Try not to feel overwhelmed, and don't give up! As you succeed, your confidence will grow. Ask your adult children and advisors to help.

When you complete a task or understand a topic, erase the star on the *Contents* page and replace it with a checkmark. You may want to note the date.

Each page has a line between the page number and title which you can also check off.

Keep referring back to the *Contents* pages, and pick a few more things to accomplish.

Set up your file cabinet right away to save the documents and paperwork that you will locate and produce (Chapter 14).

Take this book along as you work on tasks. Share it with those who can help you. An order form is on the last page for extra copies.

Contents / Checklist

(Place a checkmark next to each item as it is accomplished)

Chapter 1: THINGS TO DO RIGHT AWAY

1. ____ Keep a phone log
2. ____ Copy important mail you send
3. ____ Keep a supply of death certificates
4. ____ Deal with mail daily
5. ____ Make a "paid bill" holder box
6. ____ Cancel health supplies for deceased
7. ____ Carry an emergency contact card
8. ____ Avoid hasty money decisions
9. ____ Locate the Will
10. ____ Locate life insurance policies

Chapter 2: IMPORTANT PHONE CALLS

11. ____ Call life insurance companies
12. ____ Call Social Security
13. ____ Social Security benefits
14. ____ Call car insurance
15. ____ Contact business associates & customers
16. ____ Call Human Resources
17. ____ Call the Union and Credit Union at work
18. ____ Contact past employers
19. ____ Call the mortgage company or landlord
20. ____ Call investment companies
21. ____ Call the Annuity company
22. ____ Call credit cards to close accounts
23. ____ Call businesses to close accounts

Chapter 14: YOUR NEW FILE CABINET

98._____ Start a new file cabinet
99._____ File labeled: "Medical Statements"
100._____ "Death Certificates"
101._____ "(bank name)"
102._____ "Retirement Monthly Income"
103._____ "Pay-Stubs, Contracts, Evaluations"
104._____ "(Deceased's name) Estate"
105._____ "Portfolio / Assets"
106._____ "Investment Statements"
107._____ "Stock Transactions - This Year"
108._____ "Health Insurance"
109._____ "Long Term Care"
110._____ "Life Insurance"
111._____ "House Insurance"
112._____ "Car Insurance"
113._____ "Car"
114._____ "(your house address)"
115._____ "(rental address) Expenses / Lease"
116._____ "My Rental Home"
117._____ "Loans"
118._____ "Tax Documents - This Year"
119._____ "Tax Deductions"
120._____ "Receipts and Warranties"
121._____ "My Funeral Arrangements"
122._____ "(deceased's name) Funeral Costs"
123._____ "My Will"
124._____ "Letter of Final Instructions"
125._____ "Important Certificates"
126._____ "Open Accounts"
127._____ "Credit Reports"
128._____ "Credit Cards"
129._____ Bottom file cabinet drawer

Preface

My parents married during World War II, and nearly made it to their 59th anniversary. Dad was a doctor, and Mom looked after the home and kids.

After Dad's death, Mom felt her mind was "in a fog", and she just didn't know what to do.

It soon became evident that Mom needed help with the myriad of tasks that a surviving spouse needs to take care of.

I realized that Mom needed to get her affairs in order, organize her paperwork with a new file cabinet, develop her independence, and prepare her estate to eventually be passed on through inheritance.

In the days and weeks that followed, I began to see that we live very complex lives. We were amazed at how much there was to learn and do. By working on several tasks at a time, things got done, and Mom survived and thrived.

I noticed some interesting results as Mom kept busy taking charge of her own life. As we completed each task, a real feeling of accomplishment replaced the feelings of confusion and sadness. It also seemed that her grieving was eased and ultimately shortened.

I feel a sense of pride in having helped my mother through such a hard time. I guess I felt I owed it to her. After all, as she would often remind me, "I suffered nine months for you!"

Chapter 1: THINGS TO DO RIGHT AWAY

1. ____ Keep a phone log

After just two phone calls we realized that we would never remember the details of those calls...

Keep a phone log of important phone calls.

Buy a new "1 Subject Spiral Notebook" in the school supplies section at the store.

Write "Phone Log" on the cover with a marker.

On the inside cover, write your own home phone number and address. It will help you if you become flustered.

On the first page, write down phone numbers of family, friends, doctors, pharmacy, etc.

Start keeping a written record of important phone calls you make (and receive). Write down:

the date of the call;
the phone number you called;
the name of the person you talked to;
description of what you talked about.

Write notes as you speak with the person. It will help remind you of what you talked about.

Try to get the full name of the person you are talking to. You may have to prove that the conversation took place.

It's amazing how often you will refer back to this phone call log. Now it will be easy for you to review instructions and call back numbers.

As a reminder to write down your phone calls, you will see "(Phone Log!)" in this book.

If you are helping a parent, make ongoing copies of the phone log for your own records.

2. ____ Copy important mail you send

We had to fill out the same form three times for an insurance claim they said was never received...

Make a copy of important mail that you send. Photocopy mail that deals with any financial or legal matters related to the estate.

Keep a copy of every document that you are required to fill out and return.

Use the convenient copy machines at grocery stores or the public library. The post office may also have a copy machine.

If you would like a copy machine at home, visit an office supply or computer store and buy a mini-copier, or a "flatbed" computer printer that has a copy machine on the top (around $100). It will make excellent copies, and you don't need a computer just to make copies. If you ask, an employee can help you install the ink cartridges.

Write the address where you mailed the original onto the copy.

Mail important documents only at the post office. Use "Certified Mail with Return Receipt", or "Express Mail Next Day Delivery". Staple or paperclip the receipt from the post office onto the copy.

Your copy and postage receipt will help prove that you mailed it, and will help if you have to fill out additional forms.

A good file system will give you a place to store your photocopies of important mail and other documents (see page 24).

3. ____ Keep a supply of death certificates

We have used 9 of our 10 death certificates...

Keep a supply of death certificates on hand. Start with about 15 certificates, which will cost anywhere from $100 to $350.

Order your first set of death certificates from the mortuary that handled the funeral.

A few weeks after death, you can order them from the County Health Department, or Office of Vital Statistics at the county courthouse. Find the phone numbers in the Government pages in the front of your phone book, under "County".

Starting 3 months after the death, examine the Internet website of your State Department of Health for options to order death certificates.

You will be asked to mail or deliver official death certificates when dealing with:

    ___Social Security notification;
    ___insurance claim forms;
    ___veteran's benefits;
    ___pension survivor benefits;
    ___retirement account survivor benefits;
    ___auto title and registration;
    ___real estate title transfers;
    ___stock and mutual fund title transfers;
    ___credit card closures;
    ___banks, etc.

You can save money by asking companies if they will accept a photocopy you have made, instead of an expensive official death certificate.

Keep the certificates in the file labeled *"Death Certificates"* (page 100).

4. ____ Deal with mail daily

Mail was misplaced, bills were forgotten...

Deal with mail daily. As soon as mail arrives, put it in the same place everyday until it can be examined. Pick a good spot to put the mail, such as the kitchen counter or desk area.

Shred junk mail with personal information, such as pre-approved credit (see pg. 82). Rip other junk mail and envelopes in half through your address. Always strive to prevent identity theft.

Look at each bill and find the due date. Write the due date on the envelope. Put the bills into a special basket or bill holder with the soonest due date in front.

Send your payment at least two weeks before the due date. It is actually highly suggested that you pay your bills the next day after they arrive.

To make mailing bills easier, keep extra postage stamps at home. Get some fancy return address labels made with just your name.

Mail bills at the post office or secure mailbox.

Save bank and investment account statements in your new files (pages 101 & 105).

Put all condolence cards with their envelopes into a separate basket or shoebox.

Reduce the number of checks you have to write, by calling companies to see if you can set up automatic checking account payments.

To pay bills safely on the Internet, consider using a bank Bill-Payer service.

Now you need an easy way to store the paid bills. See the "paid bill box" on the next page.

5. ____ Make a "paid bill" holder box

We found piles of paid bills all over the house...

Make a "paid bill" holder box. Start keeping all your paid bill statements in one location. You need an easy way to find a past bill.

Find a shoebox, basket, or deep tray that will hold an open 8"x11" bill.

To pay the bill, remove the pay coupon section from the statement. Write your account number on the check, and enclose it behind the coupon. Be sure the company address shows through the envelope window.

Then, write the date and check number at the top of the remaining statement, and just drop the open statement into the "paid bill" box. Discard the envelope and advertising included with the bill. Shred anything with personal info.

Let a calendar year's worth of paid bills pile up in the box. It will be easy to find specific bills when needed.

Then after January 1st, put the piled up bills into a file you label with the year the bills were paid, such as *"2005 bills paid"*, and put it in the bottom drawer of your file cabinet. After a few years, shred the oldest bills, and reuse the file.

Start the new January paid bills in the box.

Keep this open box or basket on top of your file cabinet, or at your bill paying area. You want to have an easy location to immediately store the paid bill statements.

6. ____ Cancel health supplies for deceased

We had to cancel health supplies from four different companies...

Cancel health supplies for the deceased.

Call companies that have been providing equipment or services to the deceased. They will not stop charging you until they are informed.

You will often find a phone number on the equipment, or on the bill statement. Examine the bank checking account statement for automatic payments to health supply companies.

Monthly payment health supplies may include:
___oxygen equipment - home and portable;
___oxygen cylinder delivery;
___health alarms and monitoring;
___automatic medicine & supply shipments;
___wheelchairs;
___scooters;
___hospital beds;
___lift chairs;
___companion care;
___physical therapy;
___housekeeping, etc.

After being informed, the companies will stop deliveries, and will make an appointment to pick up equipment.

Ask for a refund for unused time, and a final statement (Phone Log!).

Be certain the monthly charges have stopped by checking the next month's bank statement.

7. ____ Avoid hasty money decisions

Mom felt the need to be generous, paying for everything...

Avoid hasty money decisions. A surviving spouse is in a very vulnerable position regarding finances. It is important not to spend or give away money impulsively.

In fact, until monthly income stabilizes, all purchases should be carefully evaluated.

Keep current on all payments for mortgage or rent, insurances, utilities, credit cards, and loans, such as car and home equity loans.

A grieving spouse can be especially vulnerable to clever salespeople. Get a second opinion if someone wants to sell you something, wants you to invest money, or provide home repairs. Don't allow the salesperson to pressure you, by telling you it is a "special price for today only". Be very firm, and insist that they allow you time to consult family or friends, or to get a second estimate.

Don't gift or loan money until your own need for the money is determined. You may find that you will be receiving less monthly income than before.

If you receive a large amount of money from an insurance settlement or inheritance, initially put the money into safe investments such as bank savings, short-term certificates of deposit, or money market funds. Wait 6 to 12 months until clear-headed, educated decisions can be made with the money.

8. ____ Carry an emergency contact card

Who will help me if I get hurt?...

Carry an emergency contact card in your purse or wallet. This is to help the police or hospital contact the people who you feel can help you, in case of emergency.

Use a lined sheet of paper or index card.

List the name and phone number of the primary person to be notified if you were hurt. This could be someone who lives with you, relatives in the same town, or a neighbor.

If your address is not correct on your driver's license, write "My current address and phone is ..." on the emergency card. If you are living in a retirement center or care facility, write down the name of the facility, and the main phone number. You could also ask at the front desk for a business card, and carry that with you.

Next, list your doctor's name and phone number. If you have a particular hospital that you wish to be taken to, write "Take me to (name) hospital".

Write on the card if you have allergies to certain medicines, or a condition that doctors should know about. Also, wear a medical alert bracelet, available from your doctor.

Other names and phone numbers could include out of town relatives, your attorney, your chosen mortuary, and the executor of your Will.

Fold up the paper and write "Emergency Contact" on the outside, and carry it with you.

9. _____ Locate the Will

Looking, looking, looking, oh, of course, in the bottom drawer...

Locate the Will. If a Will cannot be found, the distribution of property, money, and guardianship for children will be decided by State Intestate laws through the probate process.

A Will is a document that is written during life, to express a person's wishes after death.

If you have not located the Will, it may be in the possession of the deceased's lawyer, or filed with the County Clerk.

You may have to ask family members if they know where the Will is kept.

In the home, the Will may be found in a file cabinet, a safe, with personal belongings, or in a desk or dresser drawer.

The original Will should never be kept in a safe-deposit box in the bank. If the box is in the name of the deceased, the box may be sealed for quite some time without anyone being able to get into it. It is okay to keep an extra copy in a safe-deposit box, if someone else is also listed on the entry card.

Once the Will has been located, an attorney who is knowledgeable in estate law should examine the Will, and be asked if the Will should be filed with the County Superior Court for probate (see page 33). Keep a copy of the Will in the file labeled "*(deceased's name) Estate*" (page 104).

The surviving spouse's new Will should be kept in the file labeled "*My Will*" (page 123).

10. ____ Locate life insurance policies

If only there would have been a written list...

Locate life insurance policies. Look in the file cabinet, home safe or fireproof box, bank safe-deposit box, or among papers in a desk.

You may find fancy official-looking packets of paper, or as little as a single sheet of benefits.

Examine the bank statement for a monthly automatic payment.

Check for life insurance where the deceased worked. There may also be an Accidental Death and Dismemberment (AD&D) policy. Even past jobs could still have a current policy.

The surviving spouse could have a policy at work that covers the deceased spouse.

Check with the insurance companies that provided car, homeowner's, and health coverage. There may be life insurance or AD&D coverage with the same company.

Offers for life insurance often come in the mail with a bank statement or credit card bill. You should eventually check with every bank and credit card company where the deceased had an account, and ask if there is an insurance policy in the name of the deceased. Some companies provide a free small policy.

Memberships in unions and organizations may have a death benefit included in the dues.

Even loans may have a paid-in-full provision at the death of the person who took out the loan.

Check for veteran's life insurance through the Department of Veteran's Affairs (1-800-669-8477).

Chapter 2: IMPORTANT PHONE CALLS

11. _____ Call life insurance companies

Mom had the worst time satisfying the requirements of a life insurance company...

Call life insurance companies that you have located (Phone Log!). Have the deceased's social security number, and inform them of the death. Make notes in your phone log with the exact directions they give you during the phone call.

Request two of each form, because they will usually not accept corrections that you make on the form.

If the death was by "other than natural causes", check to see if the policy has "double indemnity", which doubles the benefit.

Remember to include a death certificate with the forms. Ask if they will accept a photocopy instead of an expensive official certificate.

Make a copy of every form, and save them in the file labeled *"(Deceased's name) Estate"* (page 104). If you must return the original policy, copy it before you mail it. If you do not have the original policy, request a "lost policy" form.

Mail the forms at the post office using Certified Mail with Return Receipt.

If the surviving spouse has a life insurance policy, see page 71.

12. ____ Call Social Security

We should have called Social Security sooner...

Call Social Security right away. Inform them of the passing of your loved one (Phone Log!).

The main phone number is 1-800-772-1213. Your local offices can be found in the Government pages in the front of your phone book, in the "Federal" section.

You will need the Social Security numbers for both the deceased and surviving spouse. These can be found on past tax forms.

If the deceased was retired, this call will stop his or her Social Security payments. Any money paid during the month of the death, will be taken back (recaptured). If you receive a check for the deceased after the date of death, do not cash it. Call Social Security to discuss how to return the check. If you receive a payment by direct deposit, don't spend the money, because they will eventually recapture money right out of the account.

Remember to take notes in your phone log as you speak with Social Security.

You will be asked to mail an official death certificate to Social Security.

Request handbooks that will explain benefits.

The Internet website for Social Security information is www.ssa.gov.

13. ____ Social Security benefits

They took back a payment and lowered Mom's monthly income by a third...

Social Security benefits will be determined when you call the Social Security office. They will probably tell you right on the phone if you are eligible for "Survivor Benefits".

A retired widow or widower will now start receiving a new "surviving spouse benefit". If you were both receiving payments, it is important to understand that your total monthly income will be reduced, as only the higher of your two Social Security payments will continue. You may not collect both payments.

Optional Medicare health insurance choices are deducted from your Social Security check.

A monthly benefit may be available for a surviving spouse at age 60. A divorced spouse may also be eligible.

The deceased's parents may be eligible for benefits, if the deceased provided at least half of their support.

A monthly benefit is available for a surviving spouse of any age who is caring for the deceased's child (under age 16, or disabled).

Be sure to set up direct deposit into your checking account while you are on the phone.

There is a small benefit of $255 that may be used toward funeral or other expenses.

14. ____ Call car insurance

Removing Dad from the policy lowered costs...

Call car insurance to inform them of the death (Phone Log!). The customer service phone number can be found on the proof of insurance cards or on the bill statement.

Remove the deceased's name from the policy. Wait until all claims have been completed if the death was the result of an automobile accident.

If the surviving spouse needs to continue having car insurance, discuss with the agent how you can lower the monthly payments. Raising the "Collision" and "Comprehensive" deductibles (your portion to pay for repairs) are the most common way to reduce premiums.

Consider raising the Bodily Injury Liability portion. This protects you if you are sued for causing an accident. There is usually very little extra cost to raise the liability coverage to the maximum, typically $500,000.

Ask the agent if there was a life insurance or Accidental Death policy on the deceased.

If you cannot locate your current policy, ask for a new copy. Place the policy and updates into the file labeled *"Car Insurance"* (page 112).

Set up automatic checking account payments to reduce the number of bills paid by check.

Sell extra cars, possibly to family members, and then call the insurance company to remove the cars from your insurance coverage.

15. _____ Contact business associates & customers

Dad had maintained contact with his patients...

Contact business associates and customers, if the deceased was a professional or business owner.

A list of clients or customers may be found in a database in a computer, or in the files at the office area.

Customers need to be notified if the deceased was a small business owner who provided a service, such as a tax preparer. Clients should be allowed to come pick up their records, or they may be transferred to another professional.

There may be contracts that the deceased was obligated to fulfill. An employee, professional colleague, or attorney may be able to assist.

A Partnership agreement has priority over the Will. Co-partners or co-shareholders may have first option to purchase the deceased's portion of the business.

You cannot be left a professional practice that you are not qualified to run. You will need to speak to a lawyer, and find a buyer or partner for the business.

16. ____ Call Human Resources

Mom's survivor benefit was reduced and a full payment was taken back...

Call Human Resources if the deceased was receiving retirement benefits. Report the death, and request "survivor" benefits (Phone Log!).

Be aware that a pension benefit payment for the surviving spouse will decrease, often losing as much as 55%. It is even possible that the pension may completely stop. This could be the case if the survivor benefit was originally waived to get higher payments during life.

Like Social Security, they will recapture any money that they pay out after the date of death.

Set up direct checking account deposits for your "survivor benefit" payments.

Remember to ask if there is a life insurance policy.

If the deceased was still employed, request reimbursement for remaining vacation and sick-leave days.

Check to see if there are current insurance policies at work. There may be several types of insurance, including salary, disability, accidental death, and life insurance. Discuss your options for continuing health insurance under "COBRA".

Some caring employers and staff may provide extra benefits and scholarships.

17. ____ Call the Union and Credit Union at work

The Union should be there to help...

Call the Union and Credit Union at work (Phone Log!).

At the Union, report the death, and ask if there is a life insurance benefit from membership in the Union. There may be additional death benefits for the surviving spouse and dependent children.

If the death was work-related, there may be accidental death benefits, and worker's compensation benefits.

At the Credit Union, report the death, and ask if there are life insurance benefits available.

The deceased may have had a savings account at the Credit Union. If there is an open account and you are co-owner or beneficiary, you can change the account to just your name, or withdraw the money and close the account.

If you keep the account open, be sure to change your beneficiary designation.

The deceased may have a car or personal loan at the Credit Union. The spouse or estate will still be responsible for paying off the loan.

18. ____ Contact past employers

Everyone who Dad had worked with appreciated being informed that their friend had passed...

Contact past employers to inform them of the death (Phone Log!).

Check to see if there are any retirement survivor benefits available.

The deceased may have money sitting in retirement accounts from previous jobs. As an example, a teacher who worked in several states may have retirement money in each state.

There may also be a life insurance policy that is still in effect.

19. ____ Call the mortgage company or
         landlord

Pay the mortgage or rent without interruption...

Call the mortgage company or landlord and report the death (Phone Log!).

If you are the surviving spouse and will stay in the house, assure them that you will continue to make payments. Don't miss, or be late, on any payments. If you are predicting that making the payment may be difficult, it is best to discuss it openly.

If you are on the mortgage contract with the deceased, find out the procedure to remove the deceased's name from the contract, so that just your name is on the contract. Ask if there is mortgage life insurance on the loan. Request the current payoff balance on your loan. It is nice to know how much you owe. This is also necessary if you plan to pay off the mortgage with money received from life insurance.

If you inherit a home with a mortgage, discuss your options with the mortgage holder for taking over the loan, refinancing, or selling. Get an immediate appraisal to establish your new value ("step-up in basis") of the property.

If you are renting and now need to move, find out exactly how to end the rental contract. There may be a hardship clause. There may also be state laws that will end the contract without penalty. An attorney may be needed if a landlord or manager is unreasonable.

20. _____ Call investment companies

The average investor will have accounts in several different investment companies...

Call investment companies to inform them of the death (Phone Log!).

Hopefully, you have a list of all the investment accounts. If there is no list, look for statements in a file or notebook, or watch for monthly or quarterly statements to arrive in the mail.

The statements will list the names on the accounts. If you are a co-owner, you can use the money immediately. Ask for the paperwork to remove the deceased from the account. If it is an Individual Retirement Account (IRA), ask about your options for withdrawals (see page 41). If it is a "taxable account", consult a tax specialist or financial advisor to understand the tax bill that can result from selling investments.

If you are not on the account as an owner, ask who is listed as the beneficiary.

If you are the beneficiary, discuss your options for keeping the account in your name, transferring the holdings to another account, or selling the holdings to raise cash. Inherited stocks and mutual funds get a step-up in basis (see page 35). Make a copy of the forms they send you for your _"Portfolio/Assets"_ file (page 105).

21. ____ Call the Annuity company

An annuity can provide income for life...

If the deceased owned an annuity contract, call the company that holds the annuity and report the death, (Phone Log!). Any amount paid out after the date of death may be recaptured.

An annuity is an insurance product. It may have been bought at work, through an insurance agent, or from an investment company or broker.

An annuity can provide income for a fixed period of time, the life of one person, or the lives of both spouses.

A "single life" annuity pays benefits only for the life span of the named annuitant. All benefits stop at death. (There may be a "period certain" benefit, that pays a beneficiary if the annuitant dies before a stipulated number of payments).

A "full joint and survivor" annuity pays the same amount until the death of both annuitants.

Some annuities only pay a surviving spouse two-thirds or even one-half of the amount the deceased was recciving.

If no annuity payments have been paid-out before death, the named beneficiary will recover the amount invested in the contract.

Annuities are complex investments that need to be understood. Keep the policy and updates in the *"Retirement Monthly Income"* file (page 102).

22. ____ Call credit cards to close accounts

Mom closed unused department store cards...

Call credit cards to close accounts that are in the deceased's name only (Phone Log!). The bill lists the names on the account. Phone numbers are found on the credit card, and on the bill.

If the card is only in the deceased's name, ask that they list the card as "Closed, account holder is deceased. Do not issue credit". Remember, we are trying to prevent identity theft. An account can stay open without activity for up to 10 years. Write down the instructions that customer service gives you in the phone log. You will probably have to send a letter and a death certificate. Ask if you can send a photocopy, rather than an expensive official death certificate.

If the card has both the surviving spouse and the deceased on the account, you may wish to keep the credit card open. Ask for the process to remove the deceased's name, so that only your name and social security number are listed.

Closely examine the deceased's credit reports to see all the open accounts (see page 44).

If there are balances owed on the credit cards, you may be responsible to pay off the balance before they will close the account.

Keep at least one active credit card open in the name of the surviving spouse for car rental, airplane tickets, hotel reservations, catalog and Internet purchases, and maintaining credit.

Remember to ask if there is life insurance.

23. ____ Call businesses to close accounts

Dad had several memberships we had to close...

Call businesses to close accounts that are in the deceased's name (Phone Log!).

You may find membership cards and store credit cards in the wallet or purse. Also, examine the bank statement to see if there are any automatic payments from the checking account.

Examples of accounts and memberships to close may include:

___cell phone;

___fitness club;

___membership discount store;

___video and DVD rental;

___auto clubs;

___tire stores;

___local clothing stores;

___travel service;

___camping or RV club;

___your options regarding a Time Share;

___golf country club;

___Internet provider;

___website hosting company;

___professional organizations;

___Service Organizations, Lodges;

___public library, etc.

Some memberships may be on a yearly contract. These can be very difficult to close early, but there may be a death clause. Find out exactly how to give notice to close the membership. Take notes in the phone log.

Chapter 3: THINGS TO DO SOON

24. ____ Your own file cabinet

We found files and important papers in the basement, garage boxes, and desk drawers...

It is time to set up your own file cabinet.

Many tasks in this book produce paperwork that you need to keep in a file. By having a file cabinet set up, you will have a super-organized place to put paperwork and documents as they are located and produced.

If the deceased had a file cabinet, familiarize yourself with the contents. Then transfer materials to your new personal files as needed.

In Chapter 14 *Your New File Cabinet*, page 98 discusses buying a file cabinet and setting up hanging files. Pages 99 through 128 detail the individual files discussed in this book.

See the order form at the end of this book if you would like to order a pre-labeled set of hanging files or file tabs.

Check off this page when your file cabinet is all organized.

25. ____ Change real estate to your name

Changing property title now will prevent problems in the future...

Change real estate to your name, if the home was titled jointly with you and the deceased, or if you inherit the home.

You will need to take a trip to the County office that holds property deeds. Find the phone number and location in the front of your phone book in the Government pages, in the "County" section, possibly under the "Recorder's Office", or call the County General Information phone number. They can tell you what names are on the property deed, and what paperwork they require (Phone Log!). Be sure to take an official death certificate.

There is a small charge, and easy paperwork.

Pay for a photocopy of the new property title, and place it in the file labeled *"(your house address)"* (page 114).

Adding an adult child's name onto your title is not suggested. There may be tax issues for gifting half of the property value. Also, your adult child retains your original purchase price, causing "capital gains" taxes if the property has increased in value and needs to be sold. Passing the property on through inheritance will give the heir a full "step-up in basis" to the value of the property at the date of your death.

Your new Will or Trust should clearly identify who you want to inherit specific properties.

26. _____ Get a property appraisal

Property values have certainly increased lately...

Get a property appraisal after the death of a spouse or parent. Find *"Appraisers"* in the yellow pages. The appraiser will determine the current value of real estate property. This will raise the original cost basis of the real estate for the heir or surviving spouse.

In most states, one-half of the property (the deceased spouse's share) will increase to the current value. The surviving spouse's half of the property remains at the original purchase price.

In community property states (Arizona, California, Idaho, Louisiana, Nevada, New Mexico, Texas, Washington, and Wisconsin), the surviving spouse gets a full step-up in basis on the real estate.

Establishing your new home value is important in case you have to sell the home in the future to pay for your own care. As property values increase, and tax laws change, you may be taxed on the increase in value of your home when you sell.

If you are inheriting real estate, a property appraisal is absolutely necessary. The appraisal will establish your new step-up in basis value of the home.

Keep the appraisal in your safe-deposit box, with a photocopy stored in the file labeled *"(your house address)"* (page 114).

Establish the property value now. It can be very difficult to later attempt to appraise your property back to the date of death.

27. _____ Change beneficiaries

Weeks later, Mom still had accounts with Dad as her beneficiary...

Change beneficiaries on your documents and accounts that had the deceased as your beneficiary. This can include:

   ___Life insurance policies;
   ___your job retirement plan papers;
   ___your job accidental death policy;
   ___Individual Retirement Accounts;
   ___Bank beneficiary forms;
   ___Credit Union accounts;
   ___Brokerage account beneficiary forms;
   ___each Mutual Fund company, etc.

Call or visit the locations that hold these documents. Tell them you need to change your beneficiary. A "Payable-On-Death" designation gives your beneficiary immediate access to your account, and avoids probate.

Think about who you would like to inherit the money from these accounts. The change must be made in writing on the account paperwork. It is not enough to mention beneficiaries in the Will. The name listed on the beneficiary form gets the money. It is best to list a person, as complex transfers and tax problems may result if you list your "estate" as the beneficiary.

Make a copy of each new beneficiary form, and place it into the appropriate file.

28. _____ Get at-the-door mail delivery

Mom was unable to check her mail daily...

Get at-the-door mail delivery if it is physically difficult for you to walk to your mailbox at the street.

To request at-the-door mail delivery, a letter needs to be sent to the local postmaster with a note from your doctor. The doctor has to verify that you are unable to safely check the mail daily.

Call the post office to get the address where you should send a request for "at-the-door mail delivery" (Phone Log!). This is typically to the Postmaster at your nearest post office.

Inform your doctor that you need a note requesting the service, due to your physical limitations. Make a copy of the note. Send the note with your personal letter to the Postmaster.

When you receive an okay, have someone mount a mailbox near your door. Home improvement stores carry a selection of mailboxes. Purchase a wall-mounted locking mailbox for the best security.

Now you can feel safer about getting your mail. You will also feel better about putting your bill payments in the mailbox to be picked up by the mail delivery person.

If you are not granted at-the-door delivery, ask a neighbor to help get the mail. To prevent mail theft, do not leave mail in the box overnight, and replace the street box with a locking mail box.

Chapter 4: THE DECEASED VETERAN

29. _____ Call Veterans Affairs

*Dad was a World War II veteran in the
Army Air Corp...*

Call the Department of Veterans Affairs (V.A.)
if the deceased ever served in the armed forces.

The deceased is entitled to burial benefits,
and the surviving spouse may be eligible for
Survivor Benefits Program monthly income.

The national Veterans Affairs phone number
is 1-800-827-1000 (Phone Log!). You will need
the deceased's Social Security number.

The Internet website address is www.va.gov.
This website will give information, but almost all
business takes place on the phone and through
the mail.

Your local offices and medical services can be
found in the Government pages in the front of
your phone book, in the "Federal" section, under
the "Veteran's Affairs" listing. Other "Veteran's
Organizations" can be found in the Yellow Pages.

Take careful notes in your phone log, and
follow their instructions on what to include with
the benefit claim forms that they will send you.

Photocopy the forms before mailing, and put
the copies in the file labeled *"(Deceased's name)
Estate"* (page 104). Mail the forms and the official
death certificate at the post office counter using
"Certified Mail with Return Receipt".

30. ____ Veteran's death benefits

Dad's benefits helped pay his final expenses...

A surviving spouse and dependent children may be eligible for Veteran's death benefits.

Burial benefits include:

Free burial in a National Cemetery for veteran, spouse, and dependent children;

Private cemetery burial allowance (VA form 40-1330) - $300 for funeral expenses; $300 for plot; $2,000 if death was service-related;

Free military headstone or marker;

Burial flag (which is picked up at the post office after you receive the paperwork);

Presidential Memorial Certificate.

Survivor benefits include:

"Death Pension Benefits" - monthly income for low income surviving spouse of war veteran;

Dependency and Indemnity Compensation (DIC) (VA form 21-534) - monthly benefit for surviving spouse of veteran whose death was related to service (linked to cause-of-death);

One-time "death gratuity", life insurance, and tax forgiveness if killed in line of duty.

Other Veteran's benefits include:

Retired military survivor benefits;

Health Insurance;

Life Insurance;

Home loans;

Educational assistance;

Employment services;

Unmarried dependent children also receive benefits to age 18, or age 23 if in college.

31. ___ Disability survivor benefits

Veteran's Disability can continue as another source of income for a surviving spouse...

Disability survivor benefits may be available for the surviving spouse if the deceased had been receiving veteran's disability payments.

Request from the Department of Veterans Affairs that the "disability benefits continue as a survivor benefit". Keep photocopies of the forms you will have to fill out and return in the file labeled *"Retirement Monthly Income"* (page 102).

You will have to prove that the pre-existing disability condition was linked to the cause of death. This condition must be noted on the death certificate by the doctor. If possible, inform the doctor prior to death that the condition needs to be linked to the cause of death. This will allow the surviving spouse to continue to receive a lifetime benefit. If the death has already occurred, and the condition was not noted on the doctor's certificate of death, the doctor may need to write a "Nexus Letter" to add information to the certificate of death, linking the condition as a cause of death. Keep a copy of the Nexus Letter in the file labeled *"Death Certificates"* (page 100).

Chapter 5: GETTING LEGAL HELP

32. ____ An attorney can help settle the estate

Mom only needed an attorney to write her Will...

An attorney can help settle the estate. The family lawyer, or a local estate attorney, should be asked if the Will needs to be filed, and if it is necessary to "open" Probate (Phone Log!). A Will can be hard to understand, so a close examination may be needed by the attorney.

The family lawyer will be most familiar with you, but you should be sure that he or she is competent in estate matters, and is loyal to you.

Finding a new attorney can be a daunting task, especially if you are looking in the yellow pages. Friends may have a referral, or visit the neighborhood law office. Also try the courthouse, State Bar Association, and Legal Assistance.

Ask for an initial no-charge meeting. Be fully prepared, and take the Will, Trust, current statements from banks and investments, a list of debts, and "Important Numbers" from page 43.

Be sure to understand the fees that you will be charged for in-person and telephone consultation. It is okay to visit and interview more than one attorney if you are not comfortable.

The attorney can advise on paying spouse's debts, property transfers and sales, and tax laws. There may be complex legal matters if a business is involved. If there is a Trust, discuss how it works and how to update it. A lawyer must be involved if you wish to contest the Will, or if there was a wrongful death.

33. ____ Info on Probate Court

A good Will simplifies the probate process...

Probate Court is the legal process to validate the Will. The court approves the Personal Representative (Executor) named in the Will, and oversees the distribution of assets.

Probate may not be necessary after the death of the first spouse if all property and accounts can be easily transferred to the surviving spouse. If there will be no probate, call the Clerk's Office of the County Superior Court to see if there is a state law requiring that all Wills be filed (Phone Log!). Have a copy of the Will made for your *"(Deceased's name) Estate"* file (page 104).

A more complex estate requires probate. The Will needs to be delivered to the County Superior Court. Be sure to keep a copy. The court provides "Letters Testamentary" for legal power to transfer titles and to take care of the many tasks noted on the next page. Many counties have a Simplified Probate Process for smaller estates.

If there is not a Will, an attorney will have to prepare and file documents. The probate court will appoint an Administrator, which may be the spouse, adult child, or relative, and will provide "Letters of Administration". State law guidelines then become the rules for distributing property and giving guardianship of children. It may be much more expensive for heirs if there is no Will.

At the death of the surviving spouse, probate will need to take place to close the estate. Both Wills may have to be presented to the court.

34. ____ Personal Representative tasks

This person acts for the deceased...

The duties of the Personal Representative are important and difficult. This person must please the court, the family, the beneficiaries, creditors, and the Internal Revenue Service.

Tasks of the Personal Representative include:
___notify agencies providing benefits;
___locate documents;
___notify heirs within 30 days;
___keep beneficiaries informed;
___establish checking account;
___pay continuing expenses;
___keep records of income and expenses;
___determine what debts are owed;
___present the court with list of debts;
___raise cash and pay debts;
___publish death notice for creditors;
___inventory property within 3 months;
___appraisals for property assets;
___present the court with list of assets;
___safeguard assets;
___manage risk on investments;
___deal with business interests;
___obtain legal advice and pay attorneys;
___file and pay Federal and State taxes;
___provide the court an accounting;
___title transfers;
___distribute assets to beneficiaries.

This is a partial list of tasks, and is only meant to inform you of the difficulty and potential liabilities of this job. Seek legal help.

35. ____ Inheritance

Inheritance you receive is not Federally taxable...

Individuals inherit money and property from a Will, Trust, beneficiary designation, or state guidelines if there is no Will.

If the surviving spouse inherits all the money and property, the whole estate passes outright to the spouse. This book describes tasks you can do yourself to change titles and deal with money.

The Will may name other beneficiaries. The spouse must fulfill the wishes, or contest the Will in Probate Court.

Money or property may not be available for a beneficiary named in a Will, after paying for expenses, funeral, debts, and taxes.

The value of inherited property increases to the present value at date of death. A real estate appraisal is needed to establish your new basis value (see page 26).

If the property is securing a loan, the estate or beneficiary must pay the debt or take over payments, or the property could be foreclosed or repossessed. The "debt comes with the property".

Stocks and Mutual Funds get a "step-up in basis" to the share price value at date of death, or the alternative valuation date of six months after death. Keep track of your new basis in the *"Portfolio / Assets"* file (page 105), in the Current Stock Holdings envelope.

Life Insurance lump-sum proceeds are generally inherited tax-free.

36. _____ Write a new Will

Mom needed a completely redesigned Will...

Write a new Will to make your own wishes known for distributing property at your death.

You can use the lawyer who helped you with the estate, or you can call and price other lawyers who specialize in Wills. Making a Will establishes your relationship with an attorney.

Choose a new Executor for your estate.

Using your list of assets (from page 42), decide who should inherit your money and real estate.

To distribute items of personal property to specific people, add a "binding memorandum" to the Will, or a "non-binding personal effects memorandum" to your *"My Will"* file (page 123).

If you have dependent children, choose a new guardian. A special needs child needs a *Special Needs Trust*. If you remarry, discuss how to pass estate assets to children of the first marriage.

A "Durable Power of Attorney for Healthcare", and an "Advanced Directive" or "Living Will" makes your wishes known for extreme medical care in case you become incapacitated.

A "Durable Power of Attorney for Finances/ Property" appoints someone you trust to manage your financial affairs if you cannot.

Keep the original Will in your *"My Will"* file, or in the attorney's vault with an extra copy (provided by the attorney) in the *"My Will"* file.

Discuss the advantages of writing and funding a Revocable Living Trust, to pass property to others without probate.

37. ____ Taxes

Mom was ready, and made the job easy...

Taxes are a complex issue, best left to the professionals to prepare. However, you need to be ready to provide the proper documents and receipts to your tax preparer (see page 92).

As you receive "Important Tax Documents" in the mail in January and February, keep them in the *"Tax Documents-This Year"* file (page 118).

Federal Income Tax Form 1040 is due yearly by April 15th, with extensions available. Form 1040 reports the deceased's income to the day of death, and the surviving spouse's income for the entire year.

Form 1041 is for reporting income (over $599) received for the deceased after the date of death.

Form 4810 requires the I.R.S. to promptly assess additional taxes within 18 months, to help close-out the estate and distribute assets.

Form 706 is the Estate Tax Return, for an estate value for the deceased exceeding $1.5 million in 2005, increasing to $3.5 million through 2009. However, a surviving spouse may get a "marital deduction" that defers Estate Tax until his or her death. Seek tax preparer help if you have a large estate. Form 706 needs to be filed within 9 months after the death. Make it easier for your Executor to calculate the value of your estate, by developing a list of assets (see page 42).

State laws vary, and often change, for Estate Tax and Inheritance Tax. Consult your attorney or CPA (Accountant) regarding state taxes.

Chapter 6: BANKING AND CREDIT

38. ____ Paperwork at each bank

Mom changed all her accounts to her name only...

Change paperwork at each bank that has the deceased's name on the accounts. The surviving spouse needs to visit the bank and meet with the branch manager to discuss these changes. Take an official death certificate.

___Change the accounts to just your name, and consider adding a responsible adult child to your account to help you.

___Check your beneficiary on each account. Discuss the advantages of a "Payable-On-Death" beneficiary designation to avoid probate.

___Sign a new signature card.

___Do you need to change power of attorney?

___Change beneficiaries on your bank CD's, and discuss changing them into just your name. Wait until roll-over if you will lose high interest.

___Ask about special accounts for seniors.

___Order new checks with just your name. Do not put your social security number or driver's license number on the checks.

___Get a "debit card" to use at stores, instead of writing checks.

___Open a new bank credit card in your name and Social Security number. Be sure there are no annual fees, and a low constant interest rate.

___Get information on the bank's Trust Department for services that may be right for you.

___Close small accounts, and move them into one main account at a bank close to your home. Some banks have branches in grocery stores.

39. ____ Checks and debit card

Mom absolutely loves her debit card...

Use checks and a debit card to pay different types of expenses.

Use checks when you pay a bill through the mail. Also, use checks to pay rent or mortgage, and to give money as gifts or donations.

Otherwise, use a debit card instead of writing a check to pay for groceries, shopping, and to get additional cash.

A debit card (also known as a Check Card), is available from the bank where you have a checking account. You will use a four number PIN (personal identification number) when you use your debit card.

A debit card takes money immediately out of your checking account. To keep track of your balance, write your daily debits into your check register. The monthly bank statement will also list all the debits.

Use your debit card to get cash. The safest place to get extra cash is at the grocery store checkout when paying for your groceries with your debit card. Just ask for "cash back". The Checker will help you if you ask.

Don't use a debit card for catalog purchases on the telephone and Internet. Use a regular credit card. You don't want to provide someone access to your checking account. Using your credit card will give you better legal methods to dispute a charge.

40. ____ Examine your safe-deposit box

*Mom moved her safe-deposit box to a bank
branch closer to her new retirement home...*

Examine your safe-deposit box.

Sign a new entry signature card. Consider adding an adult child to the signature card. This will give someone else access to the box contents if you need help. Keep the deceased's key, or give it to the other person for safe-keeping.

Closely examine everything in the box. Write out an inventory list. Keep the list in your file labeled *"My Will"* (page 123). Think about who you would like to inherit the valuables in the box. Add your wishes to your Will or Memorandum.

Make photocopies of licenses, certificates, documents, and car titles that you find in the box for the appropriate files in your file cabinet.

Now it is time to make the box your own. Include these items in your safe-deposit box:

___property appraisals;

___property photos & inventory (from page 74);

___your list of assets (from page 42);

___your important numbers (from page 43);

___a copy of your Will (not the only original);

___a copy of your Letter of Final Instructions
       (from page 124);

___car titles;

___birth and marriage certificates;

___an official death certificate;

___a list of computer user names/passwords;

___combinations to home and business safe;

___location of hidden valuables, etc.

41. ____ Individual Retirement Accounts

Mom changed an IRA to get a monthly check...

There are many rules when you inherit an Individual Retirement Account (IRA). Speak with the company or bank that holds the IRA to get a clear understanding of your choices. Consult a tax specialist before withdrawing money.

Withdrawals from a "Traditional" IRA are taxable as income. If you are a surviving spouse inheriting a Traditional IRA, your options include changing the account to your name, rolling-it-over to your own IRA, or leaving it as is. Each option has it's advantages. Be sure to name a new beneficiary on the IRA paperwork. Required distributions (withdrawals) begin at age 70½.

If a non-spouse inherits the Traditional IRA, rules may allow withdrawals over the heir's life expectancy, or a required full withdrawal within 5 years. Withdrawing 20% each year eases taxes.

If it is a "Roth" IRA, you might choose to change the IRA to your name, and make tax-free withdrawals. If the Roth is less than 5 years old, there is a 10% penalty for withdrawals of the profit. Be sure to name your own beneficiary.

If you inherit a 401k or other job related retirement account, the plan administrator will have your withdrawal rules. Your withdrawals will be taxed as income.

To increase your monthly income, change IRA withdrawals from quarterly to monthly. You may also withdraw more than the "minimum required distribution".

42. ____ Gather assets onto a list

See what you own, and how much you're worth...

Gather assets onto a list. Make a list of all your accounts and property, with current values. A computer word-processing program makes it easy to add and change data.

List the name of each company and the current value from your monthly statements. The headings should include:

    ___Banks;

    ___Investments;

    ___Retirement program value;

    ___Individual Retirement Accounts;

    ___Life insurance value;

    ___Real estate value;

    ___Personal property

        (insured homeowner's value);

    ___Value of a family business, etc.

Use a calculator to add up the account balances for your total assets value.

For real estate, list the address and purchase price. If you have a mortgage, note the balance and where you pay.

List the serial numbers of your savings bonds so even if they are lost, they can be cashed in.

Make a list of your current holdings of stocks and mutual funds. Note date of purchase, number of shares bought, and your cost basis. Then, you can evaluate your holdings (see page 64) and decide what to keep or sell.

Put the lists in the *"Portfolio/Assets"* file (page 105), and a photocopy in the safe-deposit box.

43. ____ List "Important Numbers"

This list can prevent your unclaimed money from going into the State Treasury...

List "Important Numbers" to have a record of all your personal and financial information.

Make a list with the following headings:

___"Will" - list the location of your Will;

___"Insurance" - list the company, account number, and phone number for:

    ___"Car Insurance"

    ___"Homeowner's Insurance"

    ___"Health Insurance"

    ___"Salary and Disability Insurance"

    ___"Long Term Care Insurance"

    ___"Life Insurance, etc."

___"Bank" - list your bank branch, phone number, type of account, and account numbers.

___"Investment Accounts" - list the names of brokers and Mutual Funds, phone numbers, and account numbers.

___"Credit Cards" - list the name of each card, account number, and customer service phone number found on the back of the credit card or on a bill statement.

Put your "Important Numbers" into your *"My Will"* file (page 123), and a photocopy into your safe-deposit box.

As accounts are added or closed, make changes to your "Important Numbers" list. At the top of your list write "Updated on (current date)". Don't forget to put an updated copy in your safe-deposit box, and shred the copy you replaced.

44. ____ Order your free credit reports

Mom found open accounts she had forgotten...

Call and order your free credit reports. These will list all of your credit cards and loans, reveal your history for paying on time, and give instructions on how to dispute inaccurate information.

As of September 2005, everyone is eligible for a free yearly credit report from each consumer credit reporting company. The three agencies have set up a *"Central Source"*. Order by phone at 1-877-322-8228. The automated voice will ask you questions regarding your name, address, social security number, and date of birth. Your report will be quickly mailed to you. To see your report online, use www.AnnualCreditReport.com.

You can order all three reports at once, but I suggest you select a single report from Experian, then 4 months later from TransUnion, then 4 months later from Equifax. This way you can monitor changes over a year. Mark your calendar for this year's order, and transfer these dates to next year's calendar to continue the process.

Order all three credit reports for the deceased at the same time. You may have to mail a formal request to the agencies with a copy of the death certificate. Then, call one of the credit companies to request a "deceased alert" be put on the deceased's social security number. This will prevent identity theft.

Examine your credit report with an adult child, financial advisor, or bank manager.

Keep reports in *"Credit Reports"* file (page 127).

45. _____ Check your credit score

Check your credit score before you need a loan...

Check your credit score along with your credit reports. All three agencies provide a score based on the information in their credit report.

A credit score tells if you are a good or bad credit risk. It is a key factor in determining whether you qualify for loans and credit cards, and what interest rate you will pay.

Credit scores are also checked by insurance companies, potential employers, and landlords.

A credit score ranges from 300 to 850, the higher the better. Your score goes up or down depending on how you handle credit.

Your score is determined by: your on-time payment history; amounts you owe; length of your credit history; amount of new credit; and types of credit you have used.

There is always a fee to order a credit score. At this time, there are only a few ways to order credit scores by telephone. Choose "score only" from Equifax at 1-877-SCORE-11, and Experian at 1-888-322-5583. Your score and explanation arrives in the mail.

Scores on the Internet are ordered at the same time you view your free credit report at www.AnnualCreditReport.com. Additional paid credit score products are available at www.myfico.com.

Keep your scores in the _"Credit Reports"_ file (page 127).

Establishing good credit and building a high credit score should be your on-going goal.

46. ____ Building your credit

*Mom maintains good credit in case she ever
needs a loan...*

Building your credit is important for everyone
of all ages. It is never too late to start establishing, improving, or repairing your credit.

If you don't have credit, start with a credit
card from your bank. Use it every month for a
couple purchases, and pay the bill early. After
six months apply for a gasoline card, and then a
retail store card a few months later. To even
further establish credit, eventually get a small
loan for a used car, appliances, or personal bank
loan. Then be sure to make every payment before
the due date. Your excellent handling of credit
will soon qualify you for the lowest interest rates
for a new car or home mortgage.

To repair your credit and credit score:
> make payments on all debts (be aware of
>   Statute of Limitations on old debt);
> completely pay off each debt (highest
>   interest rate first);
> still use the cards occasionally;
> keep balances low;
> pay bills early;
> don't open a lot of new accounts.

Adding a child to your credit card will build
credit for that child.

Avoid co-signing for another person's loan.
Their bad credit habits will also hurt your credit.
Avoid a home-equity loan, which uses your home
as collateral.

47. ____ Your responsibility for spouse's debts

You need to protect your own credit score...

Your responsibility for your spouse's debts may come down to not hurting your own credit.

Credit cards and personal loans that are in both your name and the deceased, are "joint unsecured accounts". You need to continue to make payments without interruption. Change the accounts to your name only.

Car loans and home equity loans are "joint secured accounts". Continue to make payments without interruption. Change the accounts to your name only. If payments become delinquent, the property could be repossessed or foreclosed.

If you live in a community property state (Arizona, California, Idaho, Louisiana, Nevada, New Mexico, Texas, Washington, and Wisconsin), debts are jointly owned. Change accounts to your name only, and pay off debts without interruption.

If you live in a non-community property state, the spouse is generally not liable for the other spouse's individual accounts. The creditor may try to collect from the estate of the deceased, which would reduce your inheritance.

Honor the deceased's debts, by paying off and closing credit cards that are in the deceased's name only.

For questions on specific debts of your spouse, consult a local attorney.

Chapter 7: EXPENSES AND INCOME

48. _____ Understand your spending

Mom was surprised at her total expenses...

If you understand your spending on your required expenses, you will know how much extra money you have for entertainment, travel, dining out, clothing, gifts, investments, etc.

Determine how much your regular monthly expenses total. Find these costs on last month's bank statements, check registers, and paid bills.

$\_\_\_\_\_\_\_\_\_$ mortgage or rent
$\_\_\_\_\_\_\_\_\_$ electricity
$\_\_\_\_\_\_\_\_\_$ natural gas, oil, propane
$\_\_\_\_\_\_\_\_\_$ water
$\_\_\_\_\_\_\_\_\_$ trash pickup
$\_\_\_\_\_\_\_\_\_$ other utilities
$\_\_\_\_\_\_\_\_\_$ home phone
$\_\_\_\_\_\_\_\_\_$ cell phone
$\_\_\_\_\_\_\_\_\_$ cable TV
$\_\_\_\_\_\_\_\_\_$ Internet fee
$\_\_\_\_\_\_\_\_\_$ grocery total last month
$\_\_\_\_\_\_\_\_\_$ gasoline total last month
$\_\_\_\_\_\_\_\_\_$ insurances total (car, home, life)
$\_\_\_\_\_\_\_\_\_$ 1/12th property tax
$\_\_\_\_\_\_\_\_\_$ total of all loan payments
$\_\_\_\_\_\_\_\_\_$ total credit cards payments
$\_\_\_\_\_\_\_\_\_$ total prescriptions
+ $\_\_\_\_\_\_\_\_\_$ other regular monthly bills

= $\_\_\_\_\_\_\_\_\_$ total monthly expected costs

Subtract the total expected costs from your stabilized monthly income. Now you know how much extra money you have left over.

49. ____ Reduce monthly expenses

Dad would tell us he could catch a trolley car and see a movie for 15 cents...

Now that you realize how much your required monthly bills add up to, you may need to reduce monthly expenses. Check off the line if you:
___refinance mortgage for lower payments;
___refinance to lower car payment;
___sell extra cars and remove from insurance;
___get bids to lower yard care costs;
___drop professional yard care, find free help;
___reduce insurance costs (see page 50);
___reduce telephone costs (see page 51);
___reduce Cable TV bill (see page 52);
___drop memberships and dues (see page 54);
___sell camping/RV/time shares;
___reduce credit card debt (see page 55);
___reduce dining out;
___use lower priced restaurants;
___get your senior discount;
___shop for bargains - sales and coupons;
_reduce the electric bill
   ___use low watt spiral lamp bulbs;
   ___microwave uses less power than oven;
   ___turn off lights when you leave the room;
   ___use cold or warm water in washer;
   ___hang some clothes outside to dry;
   ___use a lamp timer instead of leaving a
      light on all day;
___spread out holiday shopping over several
      months.

50. ____ Lower your insurance costs

Keep your liability coverage as high as possible...

Lower your insurance costs. Call each insurance agency to discuss lowering your premium.

The biggest reduction in premiums occur if you "raise the deductibles". This is the amount you pay before insurance takes over.

Homeowner's Insurance - Since you should not make a claim unless you have significant damage, raise your deductible to the highest amount you can afford to pay from savings as your part for major repairs. Be certain you are taking advantage of all the discounts, such as having smoke alarms, fire extinguishers, deadbolts, burglar alarm, and being a non-smoker.

Renter's Insurance - Determine exactly the value of your personal property to insure (from page 111). Get a price quote from different insurance companies and senior organizations.

Car Insurance - Raise the deductible for Collision and Comprehensive (see page 14). Ask your insurance agent if you will get lower rates by taking a safe-driver class.

There should be a discount for Car and Home if you have had no claims in several years. Some companies give a discount for good credit scores.

Insurance agents from other companies, and senior organizations such as AARP, are happy to give you their cost quote to insure with them. Be sure to compare costs for a full year. You could save a lot of money switching to a different company.

51. ____ Lower the monthly phone bill

Mom doesn't need fancy extra phone features...

Lower the monthly phone bill.

Call the phone company customer service number found on a recent bill (Phone Log!). Tell the person that you need to lower your monthly bill. You may just need "Basic Services" without any optional services such as Caller ID and Call Waiting. Instead of Voice Mail, buy an inexpensive digital answering machine.

Ask about your current long distance plan. Are there lower monthly rate plans available? Try a "per minute" rate, instead of a package rate for minutes you may never use.

Also, inform them if you want your telephone book listing changed to just your name, your last name and first initials, or to become "unlisted".

When you are on the phone with customer service, set up direct payment from your debit card or checking account to reduce the number of bills you have to pay by check.

Your cell phone may have free long distance nights and weekends. Be sure you know when your free time starts, and take advantage of this benefit.

Consider also using a prepaid long distance card. You have to dial extra numbers, but the rate can't be beat. Find the lowest per minute cost, usually found at a membership discount store. Add minutes when needed with your debit card.

52. ____ Lower the Cable TV monthly bill

Mom does fine without extra movie channels...

Lower the Cable TV monthly bill to reduce monthly expenses.

Call the Cable TV customer service phone number, which can be found on the bill (Phone Log!). Ask them if you are getting the lowest price for Cable TV service that they offer.

You may find you just need the lower-number channels (possibly called "Limited Cable"). The upper channels (possibly called "Expanded" or "Basic" Cable) triple the monthly cost.

Cancel cable movie channels. Ask how to return cable boxes and remotes, which are often rented. The cable cord then screws right into the TV or VCR, without paying extra for a cable box.

While you are on the phone, set up direct payment from your checking account or debit card to reduce the number of bills that need to be paid by check.

Some locations actually have good reception for local stations received through the antenna. Have someone help you set up your antenna to see how good your free reception is. Then you could drop cable and get TV for free, just like the good old days!

53. ____ Set up "level pay plan" for utility bills

We pay more in the Summer, less in the Winter...

See if you can set up a "level pay plan" for utility bills. If the utility offers this service, they will estimate your entire year's bill, and divide it into 12 equal payments.

Call the electric company, natural gas, water company, and other utilities and ask if you can set up level pay (Phone Log!). You can find their phone number on the bill statement.

By paying more in the summer, you will pay much less in the winter.

Once a year, the utility company will adjust your payments for the next year.

This will give you the security of knowing how much the utility will cost each month, instead of the surprise of a fluctuating bill.

While you are on the phone, set up direct payment from your checking account or debit card to reduce the number of bills that need to be paid by check.

Also, ask if there is a program to help pay the bill if you are a senior citizen, or if you are on a low fixed income.

54. ____ Stop paying unneeded dues

Dad had several professional licenses...

One way to reduce expenses is to stop paying unneeded dues.

Stop paying renewal fees for magazines, licenses, and clubs for the deceased.

If the bill is a subscription renewal for a magazine, just ignore the renewal bills. They will eventually stop. Be sure to shred the bill. You may be able to call and cancel the subscription, or switch to a magazine that interests you.

If you receive a bill to renew a professional license for the deceased, you should call the organization to inform them of the death (Phone Log!). You may be asked to submit an article or obituary for publication in their periodical about the life of your spouse or parent. This is a great honor, and you should ask how to write it, and where to mail it.

Call clubs that the deceased belonged to, and inform them of the death (Phone Log!). Ask them to stop the membership immediately, and to stop automatic payments. There may be contract issues that your attorney will need to address.

Evaluate your own extra subscriptions and memberships. You may need to stop them until your income stabilizes. Memberships on a signed contract are often difficult to stop. See if there are hardship exceptions. Find out exactly how to end the membership at the end of the contract time. Be sure to turn in your written cancellation of membership early.

55. ____ Eliminate credit card debt

Mom loves being credit card debt free...

Eliminate credit card debt to reduce monthly expenses. If you owe money on credit cards, make it a priority to pay them down to zero.

When making payments, you really need to pay more than the minimum. As an example, it would take almost 30 years to pay off a $3,000 balance if only the minimum required monthly payment was made!

Pay off the credit card with the highest interest, first. Then pay off the next highest. The bill will tell you what interest they are charging. Be sure to call each company and request a lower interest rate. Call again another time, if that particular customer service person will not help you.

Continue to make payments on every card. Don't miss payments on one card while you are paying off another.

Transfer balances from high interest cards to low interest cards.

Stop using your credit cards for everyday purchases. Use a debit card, instead. This will take the money directly out of your checking account, and will help limit spending. Control your urges to use credit for the things you want. Live within your means, and pour extra money into paying off your debt.

Once each credit card is paid off, don't cancel the card. You should keep it active to maintain and improve your credit score.

56. ____ Save monthly for property tax

If you don't save for this bill, it may be too much...

Save monthly for your property tax. It is one of your most important bills.

If you are buying or own a house, you will receive a property tax bill from your County. This bill can be paid in full, or split into two payments as specified on the bill.

If you pay the first half, there will be a second half due date. Write the due date on your wall calendar. Some counties will send you a second bill. Others include two coupons in the first bill. Keep the second bill coupon in your bill payer area with the due date written on the front of the envelope. Pay your property taxes at least three weeks before the due date. Put the paid statement in the *"(your house address)"* file (page 114).

This bill can be very difficult to pay if you are suddenly faced with a large payment on a fixed income. You need a savings account to store money that must be used just for property tax.

Open a savings account that is "attached" to your checking account. Divide your property tax bill by 12 to determine how much to save each month. Deposit this amount every month into your savings account. Then, when you write a check to pay your taxes, you can transfer the money you've been saving into your checking account to help cover the bill.

Try to get a savings account with no monthly fees, and no minimum balance requirements.

57. ____ Request a property tax discount

Mom received a property tax discount, until the County stopped the program...

Request a property tax discount if you are a senior citizen. There may also be a tax break if you are a surviving spouse on a limited income. A discount is not always available, but it is worth trying.

Contact your County property tax department to see if there is a tax reduction program. You can find the phone number in the Government pages in the front of your phone book, in the "County" section, under "Assessments", "Taxes", or "Property Taxes" (Phone Log!).

If a program is available, photocopy the form they send you before you return it, and keep it in your file labeled *"(your house address)"* (page 114).

Some counties may have as much as a 50% discount! If you receive a tax discount, recalculate your amount to save every month.

Don't get into a property tax deferral program, where you don't pay any tax at all. The state will put a tax lien on the house, and the unpaid tax bill continues to grow very fast due to the compounding yearly taxes and interest. The deferred tax bill will have to be paid back when the house is sold or inherited.

If you are concerned that a senior may forget to pay property tax, ask the County property tax department to send a notice to a family member if they have not received payment.

58. ____ Increase income

Your income needs to cover expenses...

Increase income to help pay your monthly expenses. Your income may be reduced by the loss of some of the deceased's income. Add up your stabilized monthly income from all sources, to know your total income.

Request survivor benefits from Social Security, Veteran's benefits, pension programs, etc.

Move money in low-yielding savings accounts to higher interest Money Markets in investment accounts, and "laddered" certificates of deposit, bonds, and U.S. Treasuries.

Move unproductive stocks and mutual funds into income producing securities with higher-than-average dividends (sales of stocks may have tax consequences). Consider Income type funds in no-load Mutual Funds. Then have dividend checks mailed to you.

A reverse mortgage is available if you are over age 62. The bank or mortgage company gives you monthly payments against the value of your home. The amount received must be paid back when the house is sold. This may not work well if you plan to have a relative inherit your home.

Remodel the basement into an apartment, and rent it out for income.

Find a part-time job you will enjoy.

If you are working, rebalance the number of W-4 exemptions for more take-home pay.

Consult an advisor about increasing the withdrawal amount from Retirement Accounts.

Chapter 8: TRANSPORTATION ISSUES

59. ____ Change owners on car titles

Mom put the car in her name with one easy trip...

Change owners on car titles if you are listed as the co-owner, or if the car is only in the name of the deceased.

If your cars are paid off, try to locate the ownership titles to see the names that are listed. Titles may be located in a safe-deposit box or file cabinet. If you can't find the car title, check the yearly vehicle registration for owner's names.

You will need to visit the car licensing agency in the county that the deceased lived in. You can find addresses in the government pages in front of your phone book, under "County". The listing may be under "Vehicle License", "Motor Vehicle", "Licenses", or other similar listing. You may want to try to contact a human to ask what is needed to put the car title in your name only.

Take the title if available, the yearly car registration, and an official death certificate. If you are inheriting the vehicle, you may need to take Probate Letters or the Will.

Ask if your state has a "Payable-On-Death" beneficiary designation to ease title transfers.

They will mail the new title to you, or print it while you wait. Keep the title in the safe-deposit box, or the file labeled *"Car"* (page 113).

If the car is still under a car loan or lease, the loan company needs to be called for your options on taking over the payments in your name, or paying off the loan.

60. ____ Do you really still need a car?

Mom continued to drive for a year, and then gave up driving at the retirement home...

Do you really still need a car? Your safety is important, so think carefully about your current driving skills.

Eyesight problems, arthritis, reduced reaction time, and nervousness, are signs that your driving days may be numbered.

Driving is expensive! Your monthly costs for gas, insurance, car payments, maintenance, and repairs, can really add up.

A senior can often find alternate transportation from van, bus, and volunteer drivers at Senior Centers. Check local Senior Outreach publications at the Library for other transportation sources. If your doctor will certify that you are unable to drive, you may be eligible for programs through the Metro or RTD system, such as Access-A-Ride and reduced rate Taxi. Ask about senior reduced bus passes.

Family members can be asked for occasional rides to the store for groceries or supplies (see page 87).

If you move to a retirement center, they will provide transportation to stores, entertainment, and even doctor visits.

Most importantly, you wouldn't want to hurt yourself or others because of reduced driving skills due to age and health.

61. ____ Car maintenance

Dad took care of all the car care...

Car maintenance is important for personal and passenger safety.

If you purchased a new car within the past few years, it may still be under warranty for repairs. If you are unsure, call a dealership of your car type, and they can check their records.

Look in the car manual for the maintenance schedule. The manual may be located in the glove compartment. A replacement maintenance schedule can be ordered from the dealership. Talk to the service department to discuss costs for maintenance depending on the car's mileage.

Your important car concerns are:

___gas - don't run low on gas. Fill the tank
    every time the gauge reads half-full;

___oil - have the dipstick oil level checked;

___tires - check tire pressure at a tire shop;

___brakes - the tire shop can also check the
    condition of your brakes;

___wipers - maintain good windshield wipers
    that don't streak, and full washer fluid;

___lights - check all lights and turn signals.

Gas stations with a garage will often help you check your oil and tire pressure.

Have a small memo pad in the glove compartment to write down the dates of car maintenance tasks. Keep receipts in your *"Car"* file (page 113).

To make it safer for you to change lanes, put "wide-angle spot mirrors" on your side mirrors. A car parts store worker should help if you ask.

62. ____ Registration and insurance cards

Mom was confused with the emission inspection...

Your vehicle registration certificate for license plate renewal, and required "proof of insurance" card, must be kept current in your car.

Watch for the yearly license plate renewal bill. Mail it back with a check, and you will receive the new registration, and a new sticker to cover last year's sticker on the license plate. Most states now have the current sticker just on the back license plate. Sign the registration. Shred last year's registration, and replace it with the new one. You may find the registration in the glove compartment or on the sun visor. To help prevent identity theft, it is now suggested that you keep your registration and proof of insurance cards locked in the trunk.

Emission inspections are typically required every other year. The license plate renewal will tell you if an emission test is required. You will have to take the car and renewal paperwork to an emission inspection station. Mail the passed emission test slip with your license plate renewal and check.

If you don't have enough time to renew by mail, you will have to take everything to a local Vehicle License Agency office.

Your proof of insurance card will be mailed from the car insurance company. Usually there is one card to keep in the car with the registration, and a second card to keep behind your driver's license in your wallet.

63. ____ Check your driver's license expiration

Mom noticed just in time that her license was about to expire...

Check your driver's license expiration date to see when it expires.

In most states, your driver's license expires every five years on your birthday. You need to visit your state Driver's License Examining Office before it expires. This will prevent extra fees, and a possible ticket.

You might receive a reminder notice in the mail that will have information on your options for how to renew. Senior drivers will usually have to visit a driver licensing office. Find the address in the front of the phone book in the Government pages, in the "State" section, under "Driver's License" or "Licensing".

Due to increasing security, you will probably need your Social Security number. There will be a vision test, and after a certain age, you may be required to take a driving test.

Ask if there is a safe-driving class for seniors, that will give you a discount on your insurance premiums.

If you don't drive, you still need an official ID with your photo and address. An "identification card for non-drivers" is available from the state Driver's License Examining Office.

Chapter 9: YOUR MONEY

64. ____ Evaluate your current investments

Become familiar with the stocks you own...

Evaluate your current investments by getting to know each investment in your portfolio. This will help you decide if it interests you to keep it.

Do some homework on each stock you own. Understand what the company produces. At the library, look up your stocks in the *Value Line* notebooks (see page 67). It is easy to get information on the Internet. Visit the company's website. Read news and analyst reports in the research sections on your brokers website, or other stock information sites.

If you have a broker, you could gather statements from your investment accounts, and have a meeting to discuss your holdings. Concentrate on understanding each stock and mutual fund, and if it should be held or sold. The broker may suggest lots of changes to generate commissions, but you need to make educated decisions on your own. There will be tax issues if stocks and mutual funds are sold in taxable accounts.

You may want to involve your adult children in evaluating your current investments. Perhaps they will have some recommendations as to how to consolidate your accounts, and update your holdings.

United States Savings Bonds in the name of the deceased can be cashed at a bank with a death certificate. You will owe taxes on the interest that the bond has accumulated.

65. ____ Put money into safe investments

Keep money safe for later educated decisions...

Put money into safe investments that you receive from inheritance or life insurance. Don't make immediate major financial decisions.

Have the money direct-deposited into your bank account as a lump sum. Do not have a balance of over the FDIC insurance limit (usually $100,000) in any one bank. Open additional accounts in other banks, if necessary.

The life insurance company may place your money in their money market account. Have them issue you a checkbook. Then write checks to your bank and brokerage accounts to empty the account at the insurance company. They may also try to sell you annuities, more insurance, or other investments.

A lump sum can be used for the deceased's final expenses, your pre-need funeral plan, paying off a mortgage, eliminating credit card debt, and investing. It may also be used for increasing your monthly income to pay the bills.

It is suggested that you have an emergency savings fund account. Total up your expected monthly bills (see page 48), and keep 4-8 months worth of savings available to pay the bills if your income from work should temporarily stop.

Safe investments include bank savings and Certificates of Deposit, and a Money Market account in a Mutual Fund or investment account. Treasury Notes and Bills are more sophisticated, available online at www.treasurydirect.gov.

66. _____ Open an "investment account"

Savings accounts just aren't keeping up...

Open an "investment account" at your bank, a discount brokerage, or Mutual Fund.

Some major banks have investment services. There are usually two types of investment accounts. One is a "full-service" account with higher commission fees, and a personal investment advisor who will make suggestions. The second type of account is a lower fee "computer online trading account". This is best if you can handle a computer and the Internet. With this type of account, you make your own decisions.

Deposit money into the Money Market fund in your bank investment account. Then it is easy to transfer money into your attached checking account, or to buy mutual funds, bond funds, and stocks. Money Markets pay higher interest.

Private office full-service brokers offer the most assistance at the highest commissions. They should not suggest buying and selling stocks too frequently, and not pressure you to urgently make decisions to buy "hot stocks".

Discount brokers allow trading by phone, on their online website, or in a local office. Deposits may need to be made through the mail.

Many large no-load (no commission) Mutual Funds also now have investment services where you can hold stocks and other mutual funds.

Consolidate accounts by transferring investments in other firms into one account. Transfer IRA holdings to the same type of IRA account.

67. ____ Become educated on investing

Keep a portion of money always safe, and a portion with the potential to grow...

Become educated on investing. Nobody can do a better job with your money than you!

There are excellent books available at your library on investing. See the Non-Fiction 332's section on the shelves in your library. Also, use the *Value Line* notebooks to get information on individual stocks. Look up the name of the stock in the *Summary and Index* to get the page number in the notebooks. Then examine the one page description of the stock, and the chart of past performance. For Mutual Funds, use the same procedure in the *Morningstar* notebooks.

If you would like to keep a book copy in your collection, explore the "Investing" and "Personal Finances" section in bookstores.

Community colleges offer "adult learning" classes on investing in stocks and mutual funds.

Mutual fund companies provide great informational materials on how to invest. They also have very helpful customer service advisors.

There are also excellent business talk-radio programs that discuss investing and personal finance issues.

68. _____ Financial Plan concepts

Determine your purposes for saving, and when you will need the funds...

Your financial plan should address your financial needs now and in the future.

Think about these topics individually as pieces of your whole financial puzzle.

___*cash flow* - your income balanced with your
    expenses;

___*emergency fund* - enough savings to cover
    4-8 months of expenses;

___*debt management* - controlling credit cards,
    paying all loans on time;

___*risk management* - insurances;

___*home ownership* - credit, down payment;

___*college funding* - "Coverdell" Savings, 529
    Plan, prepaid tuition plan, scholarships,
    FAFSA government grants and loans;

___*retirement planning* - work pension plan,
    IRA, government payments, all income
    sources, deciding where you will live;

___*investments* - risk tolerance, diversification,
    asset allocation;

___*tax planning* - take full advantage of credits
    and deductions, filing taxes on time;

___*elder care* - long-term care, housing, health;

___*estate planning* - current Will, Trust, update
    titles, Durable Powers of Attorney, gifting.

You can take care of most of these topics yourself, approaching agents as you need them. Consider using a "Fee-Only" Certified Financial Planner if you need help with individual topics.

69. ____ Stock Diversification Buffet Diet©

My "Stock Diversification Buffet Diet" is a fun and simple way to understand the concept of "diversification" when owning stocks.

"Diversification" reduces risk, by owning stocks in many different sectors. This prevents "putting all your eggs in one basket".

Everyone loves a buffet restaurant. Imagine each section of the buffet as a sector in the stock market. This is a "diet", because you may only choose one food (stock) from each buffet section (sector). The S & P's Global Industry Classification Standard places every stock within a sector.

Food   =   Sector   (Types of stocks)

Salads = Consumer Discretionary (Automobiles; Durables & Apparel; Hotels, Restaurants & Leisure; Media; Retailing)

Fruit = Consumer Staples (Food & Staples Retailing; Food, Beverage, & Tobacco; Household & Personal Products)

Vegetables = Health Care (Health Care Equipment & Services; Pharmaceuticals & Biotechnology)

Soup = Energy

Meat = Financials (Banks; Diversified Financials, Insurance, Real Estate)

Chicken = Information Technology (Software & Services, Technology Hardware & Equipment, Semiconductors & Semiconductor Equipment)

Seafood = Materials

Pasta = Telecommunications Services

Breads = Industrials (Capital Goods, Commercial Services & Supplies, Transportation)

Desserts = Utilities

If you would like a detailed paper on this subject, with a list of stocks in each sector, please see the order form on the last page of this book.

(The Industry Codes are reproduced with S&P's permission. Copyright © 2005 Standard & Poor's and MSCI. Reproduction of this material is prohibited without prior written permission.)

Chapter 10: INSURANCE ISSUES

70. ____ Your health insurance

Continue health insurance without interruption...

If you have health insurance at your work, call and remove the deceased from your policy after all billing has cleared (Phone Log!). Review your plan booklet, or order a new one, and put it into your *"Health Insurance"* file (page 108).

If you were on the deceased's plan, COBRA federal law entitles you to continue receiving health insurance for up to 36 months, if you pay the premiums. Contact Human Resources.

"Medicare" is a health insurance plan if you are 65 or older. Part A Hospital Insurance covers inpatient hospital care and certain follow-up care. Part B "optional" Medical Insurance covers physician services. Apply for Medicare 3 months before your 65th birthday at 1-800-MEDICARE. Internet Information is at www.medicare.gov. Examine the Medicare Advantage Plan, or within 6 months purchase the best "Medigap" coverage you can afford. These programs cover extra costs and extend covered services. Also, check on the Medicare Prescription Drug Plan.

Major pharmaceutical companies may give a drug discount, if requested. Ask your pharmacist for the phone number of your pill manufacturer.

If Private Carrier health insurance is needed, check with doctors, group health organizations, local hospitals, and insurance agents. Contact your professional organizations. The Internet can be used to search for health plans.

71. ____ Your life insurance

Insurance can provide you with peace-of-mind...

Your life insurance pays cash at your death to the beneficiary noted on the paperwork.

Life insurance can be used to pay:

> lump-sum income for dependent child;
> lump-sum income for dependent parent;
> debts and mortgage;
> funeral expenses;
> estate taxes if wealthy;
> giving money to charity, etc.

Term Insurance is the cheapest life insurance. It provides protection for a limited amount of time, and will not be available in old age.

Permanent Cash Value is quite expensive, but will last a lifetime if you can always afford the increasing premiums. There are many types of policies to investigate at your various neighborhood insurance agencies.

A senior may not be eligible for life insurance except for low value senior policies.

If you already own life insurance, call the company to see if the deceased is named as your beneficiary (see page 27). Request a "change beneficiary" form if you need to appoint a new heir for the policy. Make a photocopy of the form before you return it.

Keep all copies of forms and policy information in your *"Life Insurance"* file (page 110).

72. _____ Your disability insurance

For the working surviving spouse...

Your disability insurance policy is a form of health insurance that supplements or replaces a portion of your job wages. There are policies for both short-term and long-term disability. Keep the policy in the _"Health Insurance"_ file (page 108).

If your other sources of income or emergency savings cannot replace the loss of income, then disability insurance should be considered to help pay the monthly bills.

The benefit usually provides a monthly check for only 60-70% of your job earnings.

Your work may provide an optional disability insurance coverage at a low cost because of the group rates. Take advantage of this benefit by signing up at Human Resources.

Additional private coverage may be necessary if the job benefit would result in too much of a reduction in income. Private disability insurance is available from insurance companies.

The best policy pays benefits if the disabled person cannot work at his or her own occupation, rather than any general occupation.

Worker's Compensation is available if you are injured at work, and is tax-free. Social Security Disability is available after the fifth month. State Welfare income may also be available.

If you become disabled and have to leave work, you may elect within 60 days to continue health insurance under COBRA, however, the premiums will be significantly higher.

73. ____ Your Long Term Care insurance

The cost of nursing home care keeps going up...

Your Long Term Care insurance helps pay for living in a nursing home due to injury, illness, or aging. Payments are reduced for assisted-living and home care. There are strict rules to begin receiving benefits.

You may need this insurance if you are concerned about affording the high cost of a nursing home (approximately $5,000 per month), and if you have a family history of nursing home care.

Check with the state insurance department, senior organizations, local insurance agents, and Human Resources at your work, for companies offering policies.

The younger you begin coverage, the lower the premium payments. Also, the older you get, the more chance that health problems could reduce your eligibility. Be sure to have an idea if you are financially able to make premium payments well into your 80's. Find out how often your premiums can be adjusted (raised).

Keep paperwork in the *"Long Term Care"* file (page 109).

Medicare will only pay the first 20 days of skilled nursing care. After that, only a portion is paid to 100 days, when benefits cease.

Medicaid is a state run program that pays for custodial care when nearly all the individual's cash assets have been spent. It may be difficult to find space in a nearby quality nursing home that accepts Medicaid.

74. ____ Photograph your house and belongings

Mom now has proof of what she owns...

Photograph your house and belongings for insurance purposes.

If you had theft or a fire, could you remember everything that needed to be replaced? Insurance companies want proof of ownership and values.

If you don't have a camera, buy disposable flash cameras at the store. Begin by photographing the front and back of your house.

Take pictures of each room. Include open closets and open kitchen cabinets. Don't forget the washer/dryer and kitchen appliances.

Take a picture of the TV, stereo, computer, book shelves, furniture, antiques, curio cabinets, musical instruments, shoe racks, etc.

Then take close-up pictures of collectables, jewelry, silverware, crystal, china, and artwork.

Take a photo of each car showing the license plate, garage items, the workshop, and tools.

When you turn in the film for processing, get double prints. Place one set into the file labeled *"House Insurance"* (page 111), and the second set at a location other than your own home, such as the safe-deposit box, work, insurance office, or adult child's home.

Use a video camera to film all the items noted above. This is an excellent way to quickly show all your personal property.

Take more pictures of new items you buy.

You still need a written inventory (see pg. 111).

Chapter 11: **HOUSING CHANGES**

75. ____ Consider where you want to live

Mom loves her new retirement center, after staying a year in her house, alone...

If you will be staying in your house, follow the tasks in this book to update your property title, and to make your life safer in your home.

Your decision to move to a new home may ultimately depend on your physical needs and limitations. The steps into the house and stairs may become difficult. Some houses are just too big, requiring excessive walking. Other problems could develop from the laundry room location, and having to step into a bathtub to use the shower. House and yard upkeep may also become too difficult.

Your monthly income will probably change. You need to afford the mortgage, property taxes, insurance, and utilities.

Other reasons to move may include wanting to live closer to friends and family, moving to a home with a view, or needing a new lease on life.

Perhaps the most compelling reasons to move are if you are frightened to be alone, or if you have overwhelming memories in the house you shared with your loved one.

If you are of retirement age, take a tour of local retirement centers. Modern centers provide meals, housekeeping, activities, transportation, and health services. The monthly rent may be higher, but the peace of mind is priceless.

Should you decide to move in with an adult child, be sure to pay your own way.

76. ____ Moving to a new home

We surrounded Mom with the things she loves...

Moving to a new home can be a very positive experience. It does take some planning and help.

If you are moving to a retirement center or apartment, see if the manager has a suggestion for a reliable moving company.

Make a drawing of your new home's wall dimensions. Measure the furniture you want to keep, and see if you can fit it along the walls.

Measure the closet hanger rods, and see how many feet of clothing will fit in the new closets.

If some furniture will not be moved, place a colorful "sticky note" on each item that will stay. Pay the movers to pack and unpack. They can do it quickly, and save you lots of work.

If you move into a rental, make a detailed list of preexisting damage. List everything you can find. Give a copy to the manager. Put the original in the *"My Rental Home"* file (page 116).

Purchase renter's insurance. Your inventory list will give you an idea of how much insurance you need. Compare price quotes with several insurance companies, and groups like AARP. Price the highest "liability" coverage, for lawsuit protection if someone is hurt by your belongings.

Turn in a change of address at the post office.

Visit the Driver's License Examining Office in your new county for a change of address on your driver's license, and voter registration. If you have a handicap placard, they will also register you in your new county.

77. ____ Cleaning out your house

Mom and Dad had over 59 years of belongings...

Cleaning out your house gives you a chance to reduce your belongings to a reasonable level for your own use. It is also necessary if you will be moving to a smaller home.

Share the deceased's clothing with family, and donate or consign the remainder.

To reduce your clothes, first remove items that do not fit. Then separate clothes that you haven't worn in over a year. Do the same with shoes. Donate your extra clothes to the needy.

Examine paperwork that you find. Save all tax forms, investment account statements, and last year's bank statements. Place these items in the bottom file drawer (see page 129).

When you find important documents, place them into the correct files we have created (from pages 99-128).

Before discarding paperwork, shred anything with personal information that you would not want in the hands of a stranger. It may take a number of days to shred everything, but don't give up! By the way, kids love to shred paper.

If you are moving, it is better to reduce your belongings, and not rent a storage unit.

After moving everything you need, let family members choose what they want to keep. One method of getting a house cleaned out quickly is to hire an auction company to remove everything that is left. The auction proceeds will help offset your moving costs.

78. ____ Renting out your house

The rent on Mom's home helps pay her own rent...

Renting out your house can increase your monthly income to pay for your new home.

You may have to do some fix-ups. This could include repainting, new carpet, and a full cleaning. You may also need to replace old appliances, and possibly even the furnace and hot water heater. On the outside, you may need to repaint, and improve landscaping. Be sure decks and wood steps don't have dangerous rotted wood.

Install smoke alarms throughout the house, and a fire extinguisher in the kitchen.

Managing a rental is not an easy job. The person who will inherit the home could help manage the property. Otherwise, call a local real estate office or property management company to get details and cost for their management service (Phone Log!).

Since the house is not owner-occupied, you will have to change your homeowner's insurance to a "structure only" policy. Get the highest liability coverage they offer (perhaps $500,000). See if appropriate disaster coverage is available.

Require your renter to have Renter's Insurance to cover their personal property.

Open a separate savings account to save for property taxes and emergency repairs.

Save receipts in *"(rental address) Expenses/ Lease"* file (page 115), for yearly tax preparation.

Make a list with photos and a videotape of the existing condition, to prove damage by renters.

79. ____ Selling your home

Mom plans to pass her home on by inheritance...

Selling your home is an option if you are moving away, or if you do not plan on leaving the home to family through inheritance.

The house may need the same fix-ups as if you were renting it out. For repair work, get at least two estimates. A good appearance improves your chances for a sale at the highest price.

Choose a realtor by referrals from friends, or a local office. A realtor has resources you need, and they understand the laws. You will usually be locked in with the same realtor for at least three months. The realtor will make a current market analysis (CMA), which compares your home to similar houses that have sold in the neighborhood.

It is suggested that the house be empty when selling. It is much less disturbing for the older person, and takes the personality of the former owner out of the sale.

After the closing, prepare emotionally to give up the home. The listing agent should visit you to sign papers. The money will be available about a week after closing. Request a direct deposit to your savings account or investment account Money Market, rather than receiving a big check.

Capital Gain taxes for the sale will be reduced by the deceased's ½ step-up in basis, and the exclusion from taxes of $250,000 gain for the surviving spouse, if the home was the principal residence for 2 out of the 5 years before the sale.

Chapter 12: PERSONAL SAFETY

80. ____ Home safety

Mom never really felt safe alone at home...

Home safety needs to be a priority.

Abandon the use of cabinets and shelving that are above your reach. You should avoid climbing onto stools or chairs to reach things. Move items you use most to the bottom shelves.

Remove things that you could trip over. This includes electric cords, and area rugs that slide or have corners that are curled up. You must also nail down or remove loose carpet on stairs.

If it is getting difficult to step up due to knee, hip, or balance problems, grab-bars may need to be installed. A family member or handyman can mount grab-bars next to steps, doors, and along hallways. Bathrooms may need grab-bars next to the toilet, and in the shower or bathtub. Home improvement stores now have a wide selection of home safety equipment.

A home security system may be installed if you are afraid to be alone, or to enter an empty house. These have expensive installation, as well as monthly monitoring charges. You have to be able to leave or enter the house fairly quickly to activate or deactivate the alarm. If this is a problem, get a remote controlled system.

Health monitoring systems are available as a necklace panic button. This is important if you are unsteady. There are reasonable monthly fees.

Install smoke alarms throughout the house.

Review your Long Term Care policy to see if you can get reimbursement for safety equipment.

81. ____ Prevent identity theft

Identity theft is our fastest growing crime...

Most identity theft is caused by the loss or theft of a purse or wallet, theft of your mail, found discarded bills and financial statements, and crooked employees using your card numbers after you debit or charge at their store.

Reduce what you carry. Leave credit cards at home unless you are using it today. Never carry your social security card. Don't carry a checkbook. If it is lost or stolen, the businesses that get a check from your cancelled account could still have you arrested. Use your debit card to shop, or better yet, use cash.

To prevent mail theft, have a locking mailbox installed, available at home improvement stores.

"Opt-out" of pre-approved credit card offers. Call 1-888-5-OPTOUT from your home phone to block companies from accessing your credit files. Also, use their website at www.optoutprescreen.com.

Use a cross-cut paper shredder to destroy mail and statements (see next page).

When entering your personal numbers (PIN) at a cash machine or business, cover the number buttons with your other hand as you type in your PIN. Don't let anyone see your PIN.

Don't get tricked into giving personal info to someone who calls you. If you call a company, it is okay to give your PIN, social security number, or mother's maiden name, to prove who you are.

For Internet and telephone purchases, use your credit cards, not your debit card.

82. ____ Buy a cross-cut paper shredder

Mom's shredder is right next to her file cabinet...

Buy a cross-cut paper shredder. Consistently using a shredder is one of the best things you can do to prevent identity theft.

A "cross-cut" or "confetti-cut" shredder chops paper into smaller bits than cheaper "strip-cut" shredders.

Shred statements before you discard them. This includes any paperwork with your name, address, account numbers, and financial information.

Shred unwanted mail that identifies you, such as pre-approved credit card applications, and credit card checks.

Shred old paid bills, bank statements, and checks when you clean out your old files.

You can buy a cross-cut paper shredder at a discount or office supply store. The shredder head can be quite heavy, so be sure you can lift it off the wastebasket to empty. Better shredders have a wastebasket that can be slid out from the cabinet under the shredder head.

Put the shredder next to your bill paying area, or beside the file cabinet. You need to have easy access to it.

When the wastebasket is just half full, pour the shreds into a paper bag for safe recycling. A full basket of shreds can be very tricky to pour!

83. ____ Get a cell phone

Mom uses her cell phone if her transportation doesn't show up...

Get a cell phone if you are still driving, living alone, or are always on-the-go.

Check with out-of-town family to see which company they use. Then shop for the lowest monthly fee and phone purchase deal available. Malls now have stores for every cell phone company. Try the various phones to be sure that your fingers can work the tiny buttons. Some plans have free long distance in the late evening and all weekend. This feature can reduce your long distance bill on your home phone line. Be sure to ask how much "taxes and fees" will add to the monthly bill. Try not to sign a contract for more than one year, in case you find you don't need it. A rebate isn't worth the cost of a second year's payments.

Keep the contract in the *"Open Accounts"* file (page 126).

There are also "prepaid minutes" cell phones available. These are less expensive per month, but require more attention because minutes have to be added by credit card over the phone.

Have a grandchild program your phone book!

Carry this cell phone with you wherever you go. Use it if you have car trouble, need 911 emergency, or to call a taxi. It is also useful if you are running late. You can even carry it with you in the house. A cell phone can be an alternative to a health monitoring necklace system.

84. ____ Stop telephone sales calls

Mom's favorite saying now is, "Take this phone number off your list!"...

Stop telephone sales calls.

The caller from a sales call must be told to "remove this name and number from your list". Then immediately hang up. By saying this, you will stop those annoying telemarketers, one at a time.

To most effectively stop sales calls, add your phone numbers to the national "do-not-call list". Call 1-888-382-1222 from your home phone and cell phone, and follow directions. You can also use your computer with Internet access to post your phone number at www.donotcall.gov. If you do not have Internet access, you can ask a relative to enter your phone number, using their email address. The do-not-call list will stop most telemarketers from calling you for five years.

Some sales calls may continue, such as charities, and companies that you have done business with. It is okay to tell them to remove your phone number from their list.

Remember, give no personal information to anyone who calls you!

By the way, you may get calls from someone asking for the deceased. Since this could be a friend, it may be best to ask who is calling and why they are calling. If it is a sales call, say "remove this name and number from your list" and hang up. But if it is a friend, you can break the news gently.

Chapter 13: YOUR FUTURE

85. _____ Help with grief

Mom likes the religious moral support...

A religious leader can help with grief, and provide comfort for the surviving spouse and family. It is okay to turn to someone in a position of trust who has your best interests at heart. Discuss your feelings, and how you are adjusting to your life without your loved one. Your clergy can help honor the deceased with memorials.

If a clergy will lead the funeral services, contact him or her as soon as possible to make plans. Write down the location, date, and time of the service, and keep a copy by each phone to be sure to give the correct information to everyone. Discuss the service. Be prepared to tell the life story of the deceased for the clergy's eulogy.

There is an obligation on the part of the ministry to understand their limitations, and not give advice outside their field of expertise.

Do not become isolated. Stay in contact with friends, and increase visits. Access your religion for social support. Get even more involved. You are always welcome to visit places of worship.

If the deceased was on active duty military, a Casualty Assistance Officer will aid the spouse. A Line Officer will help explain benefits.

There are other sources for counseling and support. Your work may have a counseling benefit. Investigate support groups at the hospital, senior center, social services, and county mental health center. There are also private psychiatrist, psychologist, and counseling services.

86. ____ Reduce the deceased's belongings

Mom needed less things in sight, to remind her that Dad was gone...

Reduce the deceased's belongings, to make your home more useful and comforting to you.

Open up closet space, by letting family members choose clothing items that fit. Then donate clothes and shoes to charity. It is easier to have someone else bag up items, and drive them to the drop-off at the store. Some organizations will come to your home to pick up items.

Consignment shops may accept near-new clothing to sell for you.

You may decide to have a garage sale. These can be a lot of work, for just a little money. You will still have to donate the items that didn't sell.

Pick out jewelry and accessories to give to family as remembrances.

Consider offering power tools to interested family members. Keep a full set of hand tools for home repairs.

Clear out bathroom cabinets and drawers. Medications need to be safely disposed. If there are a lot of pills or syringes, ask your pharmacist or hospital pharmacy if you can bring them in to be destroyed.

It is important to keep items of remembrance, but it is also time to start reducing the amount of things you have. Unclutter your own life.

87. ____ Get help with shopping

Mom was driving herself to the store almost daily...

Get help with shopping. People really do like to help. The hardest part is asking.

If driving is becoming a problem for you, ask your neighbors to give you a call before they go to the grocery store. Perhaps they could pick up a few items for you, or even give you a ride.

When family members are coming over for a visit, ask them to first give you a call to see if there is anything they can pick up for you.

Have a shopping list ready. Whenever you think of something you need at the store, go to your list and write it down. When someone says they are going shopping, get your list and ask them to pick up the specific items you need.

Use coupons to reduce your costs, but don't over-purchase items just because they are on sale. You will probably now find that less food and supplies are needed.

Keep some cash in the house to reimburse everyone for groceries.

Many grocery stores provide home delivery. Ask at your favorite store for details on how to order food and supplies by phone, fax, or on their Internet website.

Be sure to use the provided transportation at senior centers, retirement homes, and transit city programs for the disabled.

88. ____ Ways to remember things

Mom was "in a fog", forgetting everything...

You need ways to remember things. It is easy to think of something important, and then forget it a few moments later.

Carry a piece of paper and small pencil in a pocket. As soon as you think of something you need to buy or do, write it down on your note. Later, you can transfer it to your shopping list in the kitchen, or onto a "things-to-do" list. Try writing individual things-to-do on "sticky notes". Stick them on the wall, and remove when done.

If you aren't carrying paper, keep repeating the item out-loud as you walk to the kitchen to write it down on your shopping list.

Instead of carrying note paper, you might purchase a mini digital recorder, or a micro cassette recorder at an office supply or computer store. Some are small enough to wear like a necklace. You just push a button and talk. Later, you can write a note as you listen to your recording. Then just rewind, and you're ready for your next thoughts to be recorded.

If you tend to forget things when you leave the house, make a list of the items you need to always take. This note can also include burglar alarm directions, and a reminder to check the stove and lights. Keep your list near the door.

This book has a lot of things to remember. Carry it with you as you go to complete a task. Remember to check off the task on the *Contents* page when you complete it.

89. ____ Wall calendar for important dates

Mom loves knowing everyone's birthday and anniversary...

Buy a wall calendar for important dates. It should have large spaces to write in appointments, and birthdays and anniversaries of family and friends. Keep a pencil near the calendar.

As soon as you make an appointment or learn of an upcoming event, write a reminder on the calendar date.

Write down birthdays (Leanne #18 b-day) and anniversaries (Connie & Dave #60 anniv).

Hang your calendar where you can check it nearly every day. Always look ahead a few weeks, so you can see upcoming events. This will also give you time to send a card.

Everyone will be very impressed that you remembered their special day.

Buy some extra greeting cards, so you will always have one available. This should include birthday, anniversary, and get-well cards. Buy extra postage stamps at the post office or grocery store.

Get a new decorative calendar in December. Transfer the dates from last year's calendar onto the new one. Be sure to update everyone's anniversary and age (now "Leanne #19 b-day").

You may even want to give filled-in calendars as gifts, especially to family members who can't seem to remember important dates!

90. ____ Get help with yard and home care

Mom needed help with all the little chores...

Get help with yard and home care

Start an ongoing list of chores that will occur every year. This includes starting or winterizing the sprinkler system and air conditioner, replacing the furnace filter, gutter cleaning, etc. You will need to find helpers for those chores if you are unable to take care of them yourself. Family members can help, or call a handyman service, as these chores and house repair jobs come up.

Lawn care can be quite expensive. Get several bids. If you already have a yard-care service, it doesn't hurt to get another bid to be sure that you are getting a good deal. You could also ask a family member or neighbor to help mow and trim bushes.

Garbage pick-up day can be quite a problem. Ask a neighbor to help with the cans.

Utility companies often provide maintenance and repair for heaters and air conditioners. Call the customer service number on the bill.

Stores that sell appliances will often have repair services. Sometimes it is cheaper to buy a new appliance than to have it repaired!

Housekeeping may now be needed. There are businesses that will give you a bid, or a private individual who just needs extra money. Even a family member may volunteer to help vacuum and clean surfaces.

91. ____ Someone needs to help with files

Mom doesn't always know which file to put the paperwork into...

Someone needs to help with your files. It can be confusing knowing which file to put specific paperwork into.

Have an adult child or good friend become aware of the file headings in your file cabinet. One way to do this is to give your helper a photocopy of this book's *Contents* page for chapter 14, "Your New File Cabinet". Another way is to take a photo of your open file cabinet, showing all the file tabs.

There will be times when you receive mail or paperwork that seems important, but you don't know which file to put it into. By talking with your helper, the two of you can decide what action should be taken, and which is the correct file in which to store the paperwork.

92. ____ Get your income taxes done

Don't worry, your tax preparer will figure it out...

Get your income taxes done in March. Allow plenty of time before the April 15th deadline.

Try to take this year's tax documents to the same tax preparer as last year. If the deceased prepared your taxes, it is time to find your own tax preparer. Ask friends who they use, and call local tax preparation companies for an estimate. There are some free services for seniors, check with a senior center or library. Be sure the tax preparer knows how to file for a deceased client.

You may need to take items from these files:

"Tax Documents - This Year" (page 118),

"Stock Transactions - This Year" (page 107),

"Tax Deductions" (page 119),

"Medical Statements" (page 99),

"(your house address)" (page 114) - (property taxes; mortgage interest; purchase, sell, and improvement statements if you sold your home).

Take an official death certificate if this is the first year's tax return after the death. You may also need to take the Will, Trust, court orders or estate plans.

Bring your copy of the prior year's tax return.

A tax bill can be overwhelming if the surviving spouse can't afford to pay. Form 9465 can be filed with the taxes to request installment payments. Be sure to pay the bill within one year.

When you get your copy of the completed tax forms back from the tax preparer, store them in the bottom file drawer (see page 129).

93. ____ Set up your pre-need funeral

Mom knows she will rest forever beside Dad...

Set up your own pre-need funeral plans, so your family does not have to make the decisions, and spend their money for your funeral. It is very easy to do, and it will guarantee that you will receive the same care as your loved one.

The mortuary and cemetery will help you set up pre-need contracts. All you have to do is call the people you have already dealt with, and ask them to make you a contract for the same things provided for the deceased. You will need to make a deposit and set up payments, or pay the contract in full. This will "lock-in" the current prices. Put the contract copies into the file labeled *"My Funeral Arrangements"* (page 121).

If you don't want to commit to a cemetery, ask your bank about a savings account that is clearly identified as a Funeral Account. You will need a second person on the account who can withdraw the money when your final arrangements need to be made. Place clear written instructions in your *"My Funeral Arrangements"* file, and ask your attorney about adding those instructions to your Will.

There may be a Society or Association in your area that gives helpful information, as well as discounts with selected mortuaries and cemeteries. Check the yellow pages under "Funeral Information".

Veterans should call the V.A. at 1-800-827-1000 to discuss your pre-need burial plans.

94. ____ Estate planning

Mom needed a new Will and title changes...

Estate planning occurs during life. It helps you pass your money and property to beneficiaries during your life through gifting, and at your death by your Will, with less family conflict.

Determine the value of your possessions and accounts (from page 42), and decide how to distribute them in a fair manner after your death.

Document your wishes. This means having a current Will, Durable Powers of Attorney for Healthcare and Property, and possibly a Revocable Living Trust (see pg. 36). If these are outdated for you, consult an attorney who specializes in estate planning.

Write your Letters of Final Instructions (see pg. 124), and develop an organized file cabinet.

Remember to re-title property and assets. To do this you need to research and see how your property and accounts are titled.

Change beneficiary designations on your life insurance policies, IRA's, and retirement plans.

If you are working, plan for your own retirement. Take advantage of your work retirement plan, and consider supplementing it with an IRA at a no-load mutual fund.

Life insurance should be considered if you are still responsible for children's education, and helping parents with financial support.

For charitable gifts, be sure to name the charity correctly in the Will, and name a secondary charity or person for backup.

95. ____ Gifting

Only gift money that you know will not be needed for your own support...

Gifting is an estate planning tool that allows you to reduce the value of your estate, by gifting money and property. Your gift can help students, newlyweds, family needing help with down payments, and as a remembrance for the deceased.

You can gift up to $11,000 (as of 2005) in one year to anyone you wish, without having to file a gift tax return on IRS Form 709.

The person who receives the money does not have to report the gift as taxable income.

If a donor gifts something other than cash, the new owner retains the donor's cost basis. Therefore, if you give $11,000 in present value of a stock, you must be sure that the person receiving the stock knows your cost basis.

You can make tax-free gifts of any amount to pay someone else's tuition or medical expenses, if you pay directly to the college or hospital.

Money gifted to a young child for college may eventually reduce chances for federal student aid and Grants. Consider setting up an investment account in your name, so the money does not show up as the parent's or child's assets. Then gift the money during college. Note the child's name as beneficiary on the account paperwork.

If you are wealthy, the person you appoint as Durable Power of Attorney for Finances should be encouraged to reduce your estate by gifting.

96. ____ A computer could be useful

Mom is fascinated by computer "magic"...

A computer could be useful for you in many ways. A person of any age can learn to use a computer. It may seem confusing at first, but by following the same steps every time, you will do just fine.

There are classes available on beginning computer skills at the public library, community college, senior center, and computer store. You could also get help from knowledgeable family.

When someone is showing you how to work the computer, write every step down, so that you can later follow the directions one at a time.

A computer can be used for:

    email (sending letters over the Internet);
    banking - transfers, checking balances;
    bill paying;
    stock and mutual fund purchases;
    prescription ordering;
    Internet shopping;
    travel planning;
    map and driving directions;
    playing card games;
    typing a book;
    making your own greeting cards.

Buying a computer and printer is confusing and expensive. Have a relative help you shop. Use a free computer at the library, senior center, or your retirement home until you feel ready to buy. Libraries often require a reservation.

97. ____ Ways to stay active

Mom is busier than ever, and lovin' it...

There are many ways to stay active after you have lost a loved one. It is important to develop your own interests and independence.

___Volunteer - schools, library, organizations;
___Join a club;
___Senior Center activities;
___Retirement Home activities;
___Theatre or music group;
___Travel with friends;
___Elderhostel - educational travel
    (1-877-426-8056 or www.elderhostel.org);
___Develop a craft or hobby;
___Work on photo albums and family tree;
___Lunch or dinner group;
___Shopping with friends;
___Learn to use a computer;
___Learn about investing;
___Work on your estate plan;
___Start writing a journal;
___Write your autobiography;
___Write a book about what you know best;
___Study interior design, change a room;
___Study landscaping, plant a new garden;
___Become more active in your religion;
___Start an exercise program;
___Study nutrition and improve your diet;
___Adopt a pet at your local animal shelter;
___Work - find a fun part-time job;
___Entrepreneurship - start a business.

Chapter 14: YOUR NEW FILE CABINET

98. ____ Start a new file cabinet

Mom's new file cabinet is all organized...

One of the best things you can do for yourself and your family is to start a new, super-organized file cabinet. It is now time for you to understand and organize your own paperwork.

Even if your spouse had a file cabinet filled with stuff in the corner of the basement, you need to start your own upstairs file cabinet.

At an office supply store, buy a nice 18" deep two-drawer file cabinet that holds hanging files. File cabinets are heavy, so get help or pick an office supply store that will deliver the cabinet. (A portable file box can be used temporarily).

Buy a box of multi-colored hanging files, and a fine-tip marker (or a label maker). Have an employee show you how to hook the enclosed tabs onto the hanging files. For a wider tab, buy a bag of "3½ inch (1/3 cut) file tabs". Write the appropriate file titles from pages 99 to 128 onto the paper inserts with the marker. (If you wish, the author will provide you with a full set of pre-labeled hanging files, or pre-labeled 1/3 cut file tabs. See the order form on the last page of this book).

Place the file cabinet in a room where you will have easy access, like the TV room or bedroom.

The top drawer is for current information, and the bottom drawer is for storage of prior years' tax files, bank statements, and paid bills.

99. ____ File labeled "Medical Statements"

Dad's medical bills kept arriving for months...

This file is for the medical statements for the deceased.

This includes:
ambulance;
emergency room care;
doctor charges;
hospital statements;
pharmacy bills;
home care;
health supplies;
equipment rentals;
co-payment receipts, etc.

Place Medicare and health insurance "do not pay" statements into the file.

This file can also be used for your own medical receipts.

Mileage may be tax deductible if you "itemize deductions". Keep track of your mileage or transportation costs to get medical care. Figure out the roundtrip mileage to your doctor, dentist, pharmacy, physical therapy, etc. Then keep a running count of how many times you visit these medical providers during the year. Also, estimate the trips that the deceased visited medical providers during the year of death.

This file may prove very useful when it is time to do Federal Income Taxes. Your tax preparer will determine if you can itemize deductions for your out-of-pocket expenses. Take this file with you when you meet with your tax preparer.

100. ____ "Death Certificates"

Mom keeps official death certificates and a few copies here...

This file is for storing the official death certificates.

Make some photocopies to send to companies that will accept a copy, rather than an expensive official death certificate.

Order more death certificates when you are down to just a few (see page 3). Keep a business card from the mortuary in this file as a reminder of who to call to reorder.

101. ____ "(bank name)"

Mom and I review her bank statement every
month over the telephone...

This file is for your monthly bank statements.

Make a separate file for each bank where you have an account. Write the name of the bank on the file tab.

Place each month's bank statement into the file. You can either staple the pages together and store them open, or keep them in the envelopes. Write the dates of the statement on the outside of the envelopes.

Check the statement for correct deposits, and proper debit and check amounts. It is always advised to balance your checkbook. If you need help checking your monthly bank statement, request at the bank that an extra copy of the monthly statement be sent to an adult child. Then you can discuss it together.

Put business cards from the branch manager and your personal banker in the file.

If you would like to keep the key to your safe-deposit box in this file, put it into an envelope with the bank location written on the front.

Other items to include in this file are:
check registers that are full,
Internet Bill Payer information,
stop-payment confirmations,
account information,
Personal Identification Numbers (PIN), etc.

Store each year's bank statements with the income tax file in the bottom file cabinet drawer.

102. _____ "Retirement Monthly Income"

For the retired surviving spouse...

This file is for the paperwork regarding your monthly income if you are retired.

This can include your:
Social Security;
company pensions;
retirement plans (401k, 403b, etc.);
Individual Retirement Account (IRA)
    such as Roth IRA, Traditional IRA,
    SIMPLE, SEP;
survivor disability payments;
annuities;
veteran's benefits;
reverse mortgage, etc.

When you receive a statement update, bring it directly to this file and compare it to last month's statement. If everything checks out okay, shred the old statement and replace it with the new.

Set up direct deposit for all monthly income sources. This is the safest way to receive income, and the quickest way to get money deposited into your account.

103. _____ "Pay-Stubs, Contracts,
                Evaluations"

For the working surviving spouse...

This file is for paperwork for your job.

Each time you receive a paycheck, put the pay-stub statement in this file. Let a year's worth of pay-stubs accumulate. Then store them in the bottom file cabinet drawer with your completed tax forms for that year.

Place your contract and other employment information in this file. This includes the current chart of salary schedules. Discard the old salary schedule when you receive a new one. This is also a good place to keep the booklet on your benefits package.

Place your job evaluations into this file. This will make them easy to find if a problem should arise.

Keep your resume' and letters of recommendation in this file.

104. ____ "(Deceased's name) Estate"

Dad had many certificates and awards...

This file is for everything that relates to the estate of the deceased.

This is also the place to save awards and certificates.

Examples of items for this file include:

___the deceased's Will;

___birth certificate;

___an official death certificate;

___information from the attorneys;

___probate papers;

___tax form copies for the estate;

___College degrees;

___Professional licenses and awards;

___Credit Report;

___Military discharge papers;

___Veteran's benefits request copies;

___Life Insurance request copies;

___social security card;

___copy of the eulogy;

___copy of the newspaper obituary;

___obituaries in professional journals;

___important letters;

___business closing contracts and papers;

___memorabilia;

___some special photos;

___eventually place the phone log here.

The deceased's Will needs to be saved, as it will probably have to be presented to the Probate Court after the death of the surviving spouse.

105. ____ "Portfolio / Assets"

This file takes the most effort to keep updated...

This file is for your current portfolio/assets statements. It is extremely handy to keep all the current statements in one place.

Store the list of assets that you generated from the task on page 42 in this file.

Examples of paperwork for this file include:
current month's investment statements;
credit union statement;
retirement plan statements;
bond and REIT statements;
social security pre-retirement statement;
ongoing list of dividends and capital gains;
information about broker/mutual fund;
information from financial advisors, etc.

Keep the statements current in this file. Compare your new statement with the old one. Then shred the old statement, and replace it with the new statement.

It is suggested to save all the statements from your taxable stock and mutual fund investment accounts. When you remove the past month's statement, instead of shredding, transfer it into the next file labeled *"Investment Statements"*.

Store your stock and mutual fund "buy" statements in this file, as well as a list of your inherited step-up in basis values. Save them in a large envelope labeled "Current Stock Holdings".

If you have investment accounts for your children, make a file for each child. Put the child's name on the file tab, e.g. *"Ben's Portfolio"*.

106. _____ "Investment Statements"

Whatever happened to the paperless society?...

This file is for storing the monthly statements from taxable investment accounts.

You may want to make a separate file for each investment company where you have an account. Write the name of the company on the file tab.

To reduce the number of statements you have to deal with, consider opening one main account at a bank investment service, discount broker, or mutual fund, and have them transfer your holdings from small accounts into one main account.

Your monthly statements contain "dividend" and "capital gain" payments during the year. Your tax preparer may need these statements for the sales of stock and mutual funds in taxable accounts (not IRA's). You may not need to save monthly investment statements if you keep a running list of all the shares purchased from re-investment of dividends and capital gains.

When the file is full, you can transfer the statements to a storage file in the bottom drawer also labeled _"Investment Statements"_. You may also choose to store them in large notebooks labeled with the dates.

107. ____ "Stock Transactions - This Year"

Stock sales must be reported each year...

This file is for the current calendar year's worth of stock or mutual fund buy and sell statements. This file is only used when you have sold taxable stocks or mutual fund shares.

About a week after you have sold, you will receive the confirmation notice statement. Find the matching buy statement for the same stock or mutual fund in your *"Portfolio / Assets"* file. Staple the two statements together, and store them in this file until tax time. If you cannot locate the buy statement, call the broker.

If you trade stocks, you should keep an ongoing list of your stock trades, including the stock symbol, date, number of shares, buy or sell price, and confirmation number provided by the broker at the time of the buy or sell.

The "basis" of a stock or mutual fund is determined by the original buy price, plus commissions, plus all the dividends and capital gains while you own the equity. It can be very difficult to come up with an exact basis. Call the broker, and ask for an "average share price".

Deliver the buy and sell statements, and your "basis" calculation totals, to your tax preparer in the year the stock or mutual fund was sold. You will pay tax on the gain, or you may be able to deduct all or part of the loss.

108. _____ "Health Insurance"

Mom keeps info on Medicare here...

This file is for your health insurance policy (from page 70). This may include your policy at work, private health insurance, Medicare, (HMO) Health Maintenance Organization, BlueCross/ BlueShield, (MSA) Medical Savings Account, etc.

Include the information booklets for medical, dental, and vision policies. If you cannot find them, call Human Resources at your job, or customer service at the insurance company, and request a new copy of your policy and booklets. Each time you receive an updated booklet, throw away the old one. Review the policy booklets. Call customer service if you don't understand your co-pays and limits of coverage (Phone Log!).

Place business cards of your doctors, dentist, and pharmacy into this file.

Keep receipts, contracts, and information for medical equipment and supplies that you buy or lease in this file.

This is a good place for your eyeglass prescription and hearing aid info.

This is also the file for your Disability Insurance paperwork and information (from page 72).

109. _____ "Long Term Care"

Hope we never have to use it, but if we do...

This file is for your Long Term Care insurance policy (from page 73).

Place a business card from the agent or agency that sold the policy into the file.

Examine the details of the policy booklet to understand the rules regarding making claims. If you do not have the information booklet, call your agent or company customer service and request a new policy booklet (Phone Log!).

It is very important for you and your family to have access to this information.

110. _____ "Life Insurance"

No one should have to search for your policies...

This file is for your life insurance policy information booklets, and the update statements on your policy value (from page 71).

Put a business card from your life insurance agent in the file.

Also include any death benefit policies you may have from banks, credit cards, work, or other sources.

If you are paying for life insurance, you need to understand what benefit or protection it is providing. If you're not sure, call customer service and ask for an explanation of the benefit (Phone Log!). Then, discuss the insurance with an advisor to see if it still meets your current needs.

If you cannot find information on your policy, request that a new policy information booklet be sent to you.

When you receive updated benefit or billing statements, shred the old statement, and replace it with the new one.

Remember to change beneficiaries on your policies, if the deceased was named as the heir to your life insurance.

111. ____ "House Insurance"

Mom has "Structure Only" on our family home, and "Renter's" on her apartment possessions...

This file is for your Homeowner's and/or Renter's Insurance policy, and your photos and inventory of your belongings.

Each time you receive an insurance renewal, compare it to the old one. Call the insurance company if they have made changes that you don't understand. Then shred the old statement.

Remember, if you have a loss of personal property due to fire or theft, you will have to prove what was lost to get fully reimbursed by insurance. Place one set of the photographs of your belongings (from page 74) into this file. You also need a written inventory list of everything you own. This sounds worse than it really is! Start a descriptive list of the items in each room. Include your actual cost, or your best estimate of the replacement cost value. Include furniture, kitchen items, collectables, hobbies, tools, etc. For appliances and electronics, list the brand, model, and serial number if possible (very useful for police if items are stolen.) Estimate the total cost of clothing, shoes, and linens. Professional appraisals and additional insurance "riders" may be needed for valuables.

Locate and save receipts in the *"Receipts and Warranties"* file (page 120).

Photocopy your inventory list, and keep a set in a location away from home, such as at work, in the safe-deposit box, or with an adult child.

112. ____ "Car Insurance"

Out with the old policy, in with the new...

This file is for your car insurance policy and renewal statements (from page 14).

Each time you receive a renewal policy, take out the old statement and compare it to the new one. Call the insurance company if they have made changes that you do not understand. Then shred the old statement.

Keep a business card for your car insurance agent in this file (and in your wallet).

Place the information booklet and any letters you receive into this file, after you have closely examined them.

113. ____ "Car"

No more searching for car repair receipts...

This file is for anything related to your cars, other than insurance.

It is suggested to keep car titles in the safe-deposit box, but place them in this file if a box is not available. Write a note telling where the titles are kept if they are in a different location.

Keep all the contract papers you signed when you bought your car in this file. This will include details of your car loan or lease.

If you purchased an extended warranty with your new car, keep the booklet and maintenance receipts together in this file. If you eventually need warranty repair work, you may have to prove that you took care of scheduled maintenance.

Place your car maintenance receipts into this file. This includes oil changes, tune-ups, brakes, windshield wipers, etc. (from page 61).

Put receipts and warranties for tires, battery, and car repairs in this file.

114. ____ "(your house address)"

Mom keeps everything about her house here...

This file is for everything related to the property listed on this file label. If you own more than one property, such as a vacation home or investment rentals, make a file with each address.

Items for this file include:

____paid property tax bill statements;
____Senior property tax reduction form;
____County official property value notices;
____copy of deed - from County records;
____purchase settlement statements;
____mortgage contract;
____updates from mortgage company;
____mortgage payment & interest schedule;
____copy of appraisal for land and house;
____Title Insurance;
____neighborhood covenants;
____map plot of property lines;
____architect and builder information,
____home improvements, etc.

Save receipts for major home improvements to your house. Improvements are added to your purchase price when the property is sold. Home improvements include: kitchen remodel, furnace, house additions, windows, fencing, landscaping, sidewalks, driveway, pool, etc. Save improvement receipts for as long as you own your home. This will make it easy for you to locate receipts if you need warranty repairs.

If the property is sold, store this file with the income taxes for the year it was sold.

115. ____ "(rental address) Expenses/ Lease"

Have a separate file for each rental property...

This file is for your tax deductible expenses to maintain your rental property (from page 78), and the rental lease contract signed by your tenant.

Save the receipts and bills that will justify tax deductions to reduce your rental income.

Expenses that may be deducted on Form 1040 Schedule E include:

___advertising;

___auto and travel;

___cleaning and maintenance;

___insurance;

___legal and professional fees;

___management fees;

___mortgage and other interest;

___repairs;

___supplies;

___taxes;

___utilities;

___property depreciation.

Consult with a tax specialist to clearly understand the expenses you can deduct. Add up your costs in each type of Expense, and identify the totals to your tax preparer. Each year remove the receipts from this file and store with the taxes for that year.

Keep a yearly listing of the date and amount of each rent payment that your tenant makes.

Also, keep the list of existing damages that you have worked up with the tenant in this file.

116. ____ "My Rental Home"

Everything about Mom's new retirement home is kept here...

This file is for everything related to living in a rental, such as a house, apartment, retirement home, assisted-living facility, or nursing home.

Place your lease contract in the file. Be clear about how to give notice before moving out.

Put your rules information in the file. Be sure to understand your responsibilities for yard care and home maintenance. Ask who to call in case you need help.

You should always make a move-in list of pre-existing damages (from page 76). Keep the list in this file, and give a copy to the landlord or manager. Find out what you will have to do to get your damage or cleaning deposit back when you move.

Receipts should be saved for your moving expenses. They may be tax deductible.

Keep receipts for repairs and improvements to your rental in the file. Ask about getting reimbursed for the money you spend.

Remember, your *"House Insurance"* file (page 111) is for your Renter's Insurance policy statement, photos of personal property, and detailed inventory list.

117. ____ "Loans"

Loan information needs to be easily found...

This is the file for the contract paperwork and information for each of your loans.

This can include:

home equity loans;

bank and business loans;

credit union loans;

personal loans, etc.

For reference, place one of the loan payment statements in this file from your paid-bill box.

Car loan information should be kept in the file labeled *"Car"*, but place a payment statement in this file.

Mortgage loan information should be kept in the file labeled *"(your house address)"*, but place a payment statement in this file.

If you owe money to someone, write a note telling who you owe money to, how to reach them, and the amount of the loan. Keep a list of the dates and check numbers of your payments.

If anyone owes you money, put the original evidence of that debt in this file. This may be an IOU or promissory note. Keep an ongoing record of the dates and amount of payments received.

When you have paid off a loan, put the statement from the loan company that your loan is paid in full into the file.

It is important to have your loan information in one location. At your death, the executor of your Will must first pay off your debts, before your beneficiaries can receive their inheritance.

118. ____ "Tax Documents - This Year"

*Mom didn't misplace a single important
document for her first taxes...*

This file is for the yearly tax documents that you will receive every January and February, in envelopes marked "Important Tax Documents". Save these envelopes and documents in this file.

You will receive different tax documents from work, banks, investment companies, government income sources, annuity payments, retirement account distributions, IRA contributions, and your mortgage holder.

Student's may receive tax documents for paid student-loan interest, tuition and fees, and state tuition program contributions.

In March, make an appointment with a tax specialist to fill out the complicated tax forms (see page 92).

You will need to take an official death certificate for the year that the deceased passed away. Go ahead and put one in this file right away.

When you go to have your taxes prepared, take all of these documents from this file. Leave the empty file in its place in the top file cabinet drawer for next year's tax documents.

After your taxes are done, store the Important Tax Documents you have removed from this file in the bottom file drawer with your copies of the tax forms.

119. _____ "Tax Deductions"

Mom has started saving deductible receipts...

This file is for saving receipts that you will give to your tax preparer if you "itemize deductions" on Schedule A of your Income Taxes.

Listed below are examples of deductible <u>out-of-pocket</u> expenses (there are more examples and limitations that should be discussed with your tax preparer):

    Medical and dental expenses
        doctor, clinic, hospital, labs, therapy
        prescription medicines
        health insurance premiums and co-pays
        mileage to clinics and back home
        Long Term Care premiums based on age
    Taxes you paid
        state income or sales taxes
        real estate property taxes
        automobile license plate fee for car value
    Interest you paid
        mortgage interest
        home equity loan interest
        home construction loan interest
        home improvement loan interest
    Gifts to charity
        cash and personal property
        mileage for volunteer services
    Casualty and theft losses
        sudden and unexpected damage
        costs beyond insurance reimbursement
    Job unreimbursed expenses; union dues
    Educational costs (unreimbursed)
        to maintain or improve current job skills

120. _____ "Receipts and Warranties"

Where did that new toaster receipt go?...

This file is for saving receipts for new purchases, and for older receipts that justify your insurance inventory.

Keep receipts of items that you may need to return, or that require you to keep the receipt in case of warranty repair.

Receipts to save include:
    appliances;
    battery and electric powered items;
    computer equipment and software;
    furniture;
    watches and jewelry;
    clothing, etc.

Keep instruction booklets and warranty information that come with new appliances and electronics in this file.

Also, set up a "receipt box" to temporarily save receipts from grocery and drug stores. Find a cigar-box sized container, and drop receipts from stores into it. Now it will be easy to find the receipt in case something needs to be returned. After a couple months, throw away old receipts. Shred the receipt if it has personal information on it, such as your name and debit card number.

121. _____ "My Funeral Arrangements"

Mom is comfortable knowing her final resting place...

This file is for your own pre-need funeral contracts or arrangements (from page 93).

Place business cards and any correspondence you may receive from the mortuary and cemetery into this file.

If you have saved money in some other way for your final expenses, put very detailed instructions into this file. This may include a separate savings account, an insurance policy, Savings Bonds, or a specific stock in a brokerage account. Consider also adding this information to your Will.

If you have a family plot that you wish to be buried in, leave instructions as to the location of the cemetery and plot space. You should contact the cemetery for a pre-need contract, pre-paid marker, and suggestions for mortuary services.

If you were a Veteran and wish to be buried in a national cemetery, note your pre-arranged V.A. burial plans, and instructions to contact Veterans Affairs (see pages 29-31).

Write down any alternative wishes you may have, such as a desire for cremation and scattering in a specific location. A notation in your Will may help prevent family conflict.

Leave a note in this file referring to your _"Letter of Final Instructions"_ file (see page 124).

Make sure that your family and Executor of your Will know of this file.

122. _____ "(deceased's name) Funeral Costs"

Dad's funeral costs sure added up...

This file is for the contracts and receipts for the deceased's mortuary, cemetery, funeral, and reception costs.

There should be separate contract paperwork for mortuary services and cemetery services. If the contracts cannot be found, call the cemetery for a copy of their contract. They should be able to identify who provided the mortuary services. Some cemeteries may have also provided the mortuary services.

Keep business cards from the mortuary and cemetery. Remember, you can order additional official death certificates from the mortuary.

Store receipts in this file for businesses that provided services for the funeral, such as the florist, caterer, and transportation.

If you are paying on a loan for final expenses, move the paperwork from _"Loans"_ to this file when the loan is paid off.

123. _____ "My Will"

Mom's new Will is easy to find...

This file is for your own Will (from page 36), and other important estate lists.

Keep the original Will here, unless you store the original in your attorney's vault. In that case, keep an extra copy (provided by the attorney) in this file, with a clear note telling the location of the original.

Place the codicil, "binding memorandum", or "non-binding personal effects memorandum" in this file, to distribute specific items to family and friends.

Your Trust documents should also be stored with the Will.

Other documents to keep in this file include:

    Powers of Attorney paperwork;

    safe-deposit box inventory (from page 40);

    your "Important Numbers" (from page 43);

    instructions for pet guardian and care;

    paperwork for family business succession.

Place your current attorney's business card and correspondence into the file.

Remember, you need a new Will now, if the deceased was the Executor and main beneficiary on your old Will, or if your Will is outdated.

Be sure to inform your family and Executor of this location of your Will.

124. _____ "Letter of Final Instructions"

Your letter should be a work-in-progress...

This is the file for your Letter of Final Instructions. This is a document that you write, telling your personal instructions and final wishes to your family and Personal Representative.

Think of this as a road map that others can follow to find the people, paperwork, and tasks that you feel need to be done after you die.

This letter works well as a list. This can be as simple as writing, "1. Be sure to call..." "2. You can rely on..." You can always add more topics.

Include a list of names and phone numbers (or the business cards) for your lawyer, accountant, tax preparer, personal banker, insurance agents, etc.

There are many topics to include:

_____a personal message to loved-ones;

_____names and phone numbers of family;

_____friends you would want informed;

_____who to rely on for advice & assistance;

_____instructions for care of the house;

_____instructions for care of pets;

_____closing your business interests;

_____handling your investments;

_____organizations you belong to;

_____list of suggested gifts to special people;

_____historical significance of antiques;

_____a written autobiography of your life;

_____a copy of this book, etc.

This letter should be an ongoing project of love.

125. _____ "Important Certificates"

Mom's certificates are all within reach...

This file is for your important certificates.
Types of certificates for this file include:
> your Social Security card;
> Passport;
> College degrees;
> teaching certificate;
> professional licenses;
> awards;
> organization and club certificates;
> Military discharge papers, etc.

It is suggested to keep your original birth and marriage certificates in a safe-deposit box. Put a note in this file telling where the originals are located. If there is danger of home burglary in your area, keep your Social Security card in the safe-deposit box.

Official birth certificate copies are available from the state or county Public Health office.

Marriage certificate copies are available from the state Vital Statistics office, or office of the County Clerk in the county where the marriage license was issued.

Give your grown children their original birth certificates. Remind them to make an _"Important Certificates"_ file!

126. _____ "Open Accounts"

We are still finding open accounts that we didn't know existed...

This file is to identify your open accounts.

Place one of the paid bill statements, and the contract if available, for every account that is open in your name into this file.

This should include:

___utilities;

___cell phone;

___credit cards;

___store accounts;

___membership dues, etc.

As accounts are closed, remove the statement from this file. As accounts are opened, add a paid bill statement to this file.

By closely examining your credit report, you will see all the credit accounts that you have open (see pages 44 and 127).

This file will make it easier to close accounts in the future.

127. ____ "Credit Reports"

Keep checking your credit reports as one method of catching identity theft...

This file is for your credit reports from Equifax, Experian, and TransUnion. Order a new free credit report every year from each agency. Try the technique of ordering from a different agency every 4 months, as discussed on page 44.

The reports will show all your open accounts. You can then call or write companies to close unused accounts (Phone Log!).

If there is a problem, call the agency, and then follow the directions with the credit report to submit written notice. You will need the report number or file number listed on the first page of the credit report to get customer service.

If you have been the victim of identity theft, call each credit agency and place "fraud alerts" on your Social Security number. You will need to order credit reports more often, and watch for new accounts. There are also Internet credit monitoring services available from each agency.

When you get a new credit report, compare it with the old one from the same agency. If there are recent accounts that have been opened without your knowledge, call the credit agency that sent you the report. It is always possible that a credit card has just changed names. Shred the old credit report and replace it with the new one.

Also, put the paperwork for your credit score into this file (from page 45).

128. ____ "Credit Cards"

Make it easy to identify your credit cards...

This file is for your credit card information.

From your "Important Numbers", write a list for this file with each card type, account number, and customer service phone number.

One way to easily document all your cards is to line them up on a copy machine, and make two photocopies of the fronts, and then the backs. Put a set in this file, and a set in your safe-deposit box.

For reference, put a billing statement from your "paid bill box" into this file for each credit card you use. The statement shows your interest rate, and instructions on how to report a billing mistake. If charges appear on your bill that are wrong, first call customer service (Phone Log!), and then follow the instructions on the back of the statement for submitting written notice to dispute a charge.

Save the benefits booklet. This will detail your benefits for rebates, air travel mileage, travel assistance, warranty services, insurance, etc.

The importance of this file becomes evident if your credit cards are lost or stolen. By having paperwork on the cards you own, it will be easy to call customer service for each card that was lost or stolen, and immediately report the loss.

129. _____ Bottom file cabinet drawer

Mom can easily find past taxes, bank statements, and bills...

The bottom file cabinet drawer is for storage of past year's items.

"200(5) Income Tax" - Keep your copy of each year's tax forms in a file with the correct year on the tab. Also, store the year's "Important Tax Documents", pay-stubs, bank statements, check registers, receipts that justify deductions, and stock buy/sell statements. The IRS suggests keeping tax forms for just 6 years. Since we keep so much information with taxes, I suggest keeping tax files permanently.

"200(5) Paid Bills" - After January 1st of each year, take all the paid bills out of the "paid bills box" and place them into a file marked with the correct year. Next year, make another file for the next pile of paid bills. After a few years, shred the oldest paid bills, and reuse the file for the next year.

"Investment Statements" - For storage of taxable account statements.

Keep extra hanging files and tabs in the bottom drawer, so that you can easily make new files when you need them.

Afterword

The information presented in this book was developed from the author's experiences. You will have your own set of tasks to accomplish, based on the complexity of your life, and the life and estate of the deceased.

If you have lost your spouse, your healing will come with the passage of time, the help of family and friends, and your feelings of accomplishment from being successful. Make a goal to work on a task nearly every day. Get motivated, and get things done.

If you are an adult child who has lost one parent and are helping the other, thank you for leading your parent through a very difficult time. Anything you do now will make things easier for you in the future.

If you have lost your last parent, I wish you success closing the estate. Always remember the good times.

Your comments are welcome. Please email the author at: MBurns@SeaStarPublishing.com, or mail to:

Sea Star Publishing
Attn: Michael Burns

21637 3rd Ave. S.
Normandy Park WA 98198

About the Author
Michael Burns lives in Normandy Park, Washington, on a bluff above Puget Sound. He has been a Special Education teacher, School Library Media Specialist, and has a Graduate Certificate in Personal Financial Planning.

Order Form On Reverse Side

Order Form

To order additional copies of *Death Did Us Part,*

1. Photocopy and mail the information below
2. Order on Internet website: www.SeaStarPublishing.com
3. Phone:
206-878-6926

Ship my books to:

Name____

Address____

City_____________________________State______ Zip__________

Email address ____

Please rush me ______ copies of
Death Did Us Part @ $17.95 each $____________

Priority Mail Postage and Handling for books:
$ 4.00 for 1st book; $ 2.00 each additional $____________

Additional products . . . . $____________
_____ Full set of hanging files with preprinted labels -
       $40.00 plus $12.00 shipping = $52.00 total
_____ 3½" hanging file tabs with preprinted labels
       (does not include hanging files) = $20.00 total
_____ Report on Stock Diversification Buffet = $10.00 total

                    Subtotal . . . . . . $____________

WA state residents add 8.8% sales tax $____________
  (Postage and tax may vary depending on current rates)

                Total amount enclosed . . . . . . $____________
Make checks payable to: Sea Star Publishing
Mail order form or invoice and full payment to:

       Sea Star Publishing
       21637 3rd Ave. S.
       Normandy Park WA 98198

_____ **Please autograph my book!** Personalize to (name):